LIFE MANIA

Southern Sudan;
A nation in the face of the Struggle for Liberation;
the journey of pain, grief, suffering and struggle for success –
a true life history of an ordinary person from South Sudan.

John Sunday Martin

A Note from the Publisher

The publisher wishes to acknowledge and thank Dr Douglas H. Johnson for his invaluable help and support for Africa World Books and its mission of preserving and promoting African cultural and literary traditions and history. Dr Johnson and fellow historians have been instrumental in ensuring that African people remain connected to their past and their identity. Africa World Books is proud to carry on this mission.

ISBN 978-0-6485028-6-9
© John Sunday Martin

All rights reserved. No part of this publication may be reproduced, stored in a retrieval system, or transmitted, in any form, or by any means, electronic, mechanical, photocopying, recording or otherwise, without the prior permission of the publishers.
This book is sold subject to the conditions that it shall not, by way of trade or otherwise, be lent, re-sold, hired out or otherwise circulated without the publisher's prior consent in any form of binding or cover other than in which it is published and without a similar condition including the condition being imposed on the subsequent purchaser.
Africa World Books Pty. Ltd.

As I recall how great my mother and father have been to me, and how they struggled to raise me (though God took them before they could see the fruit of their offspring); I discover that there is nothing I can do for them other than writing this book, to honour their memories.

This book, *Life Mania* is written to support the works of charity in memory of my late parents -Cecilia Ada and Martin Friday Jacob.

Indeed,

It is very difficult to remember those in pathetic states of life in our today's society – not because we don't have emotions or feelings,

But because our sensibilities are taken into custody by pride of selfishness to be better than others.

If you are human, then don't pretend, because you do have your own stories that could be either 'good' or 'pathetic.'

Just try to recall a moment in your life that someone came in for you -helped you without selfish reservations; recall that moment, think about it.

Supposedly, if that person was selfish and declined helping you, what would have been your state by then or now?

We all have been credited with good things to pay to our society for what others have done for us.

For this, I gave my first hand, *Life Mania* for charity works.

Dedication

I dedicate this book to all orphans and widows; that in one way or the other, may be experiencing the unexpected in their lives that none of them ever wished for. In life, there are inevitably ups and downs. However, don't be discouraged – just remain focused and determined, respect your values and be loyal to others; forgive and forget the wrongs that have been done to you – and you will succeed despite the many challenges you may encounter throughout your journey.

Acknowledgements

Success is one thing that you can't achieve alone. You need others to be part of you, and you to be part of them. Together, you will be successful though all the praises will go to you for the great achievement – which, without others, you won't achieve.

This book is in your hand, not because of my own efforts alone, but because of those who are dear to me, who have encouraged me and challenged me; those who have stood by me and with me through every difficulty that I have faced. Special thanks to my beloved Aunt Jacqueline Jacobs who never left me alone but has supported me in all aspects of life. Hannelie Du Toit – who became a fountain of hope for me and whose caring and loving touch remains a hug specially credited. Her spiritual and technical support for me will always remain unforgettable.

Special thanks to Faizel Badrodeen for the great support he rendered for my upkeep and welfare in the Republic of South Africa. In you, I saw an angel. You demonstrated to me that, in order to help – you never have to think twice– but just do it without any affiliation to conditions. Many thanks to late Arckangle Bashir Bay, late Night Noel Bunyimuki and Right Patrick Taban – the people who remained with us after the death of our father and whose support was impeccable – without such support, we would never have made it. The three of you are my heroes.

I cannot forget my dear sisters Vivian Lucia and Nancy Chukuna, as well my brothers, Tia Martin and Aku Martin. I consider them a great gift from God. They gave me the hope I needed to survive through encouraging me and praying for me.

I want to immensely thank my mentor Sheikh Ahmed Abdurrahman of Somali's national. I thank you not for exposing me to discover that unique World of Mafias; but for leading me to the realisation of my inner being and my potentialities to survive and share my life for the profit of others, my God and to be a team player. One of my greatest discoveries from your life is that, in order to be successful, one needs others to be part of his/ her own life – and to avoid selfishness with life and resources. To be successful, one needs not only those that he/ she can control, but also those that can challenge him/ her to explore their innate full potential – challenge to you increases your strength and zeal to do better. Indeed, for you to be successful, you definitely have to try your life – because life is full of trials – for it is through trying that you become a master, and then successful in life.

Special thanks to Ms. Patricia Bahlekazi for holding my hand and walking with me in life as a mother and a friend. Through you, I have learnt that, we will never make it in life - if there is no one to stand by our side the same way you have stood by my side in every moment of my life.

To all those that I have mentioned here, I hope you will come to the understanding that – this comes from the bottom of my heart, with a great love. I hope from this alone, you will come to know, how much you all mean to me.

PREFACE

The ultimate end of life is death. But those who are still alive have a chance to better their lives despite the loss of a dear one, or suffering brought about by loss. Those still alive can live and have a better life and future, despite the death of their dear one and suffering imposed by death on them.

This book, *Life Mania* is absolutely for those who have lost a dear one, particularly parent(s) to death, and those who struggle for a better life and future. It is the narration of an ordinary person, who lost his father at the age of eleven during a South Sudan civil war; his journey as an orphan through hell and his determination to succeed in life.

Through birth, we came into existence, and through death we may cease to exist; we will not all die at the same time, or in the same way, but when that time comes, we will eventually die. We are just waiting for our own specific time because no person will escape death in this life; even Jesus Christ whom Christians believe- to be God the Son, He never escaped death at the cross. He died a miserable death, like a criminal on the cross.

Of course, death is not a surprise because we all know that it will happen to us at any time. Yet, it seems that, most of us are not prepared for it. When death comes and takes one of our family members, we often remain vulnerable and exposed to pain, grief and suffering. However, these challenges you might have been exposed to because of the death of somebody dear to you, might not cost you your life and future. These challenges are there as part of the new journey of life you will go through without them. The pain, grief and suffering are there to remind you about the "late" in this new journey of life and to make you stronger and more determined in life.

You need to have courage in all this pain, grief and suffering you are going through, in order to remain strong – and determined in life. In fact, the absence of courage when you are faced with difficulties will result to your failure in life simply because it will affect your thinking capacity which will make you to forget focussing on the greatness of your inner being in achieving certainties in life. Without courage, your thinking is refocused by pains, grief and suffering in your outer being and visible circumstances, and this will limit your potentiality for achieving greatness, to do what you are capable of. Above all, without courage, you will have a negative image of yourself as an orphan, or as a person without anybody to help or provide for.

'The Life Mania' is a record of the demise of my father, Mr. Martin F. Jacobs, and my mother, Cecilia Ada. It is about my new journey in life without a father to provide for me, a mother to chitchat with and walk with. 'The Life Mania' is about my own new journey of grief, pain, suffering and struggle for a better life and future. This book will encourage and strengthen you to go through such a journey to the very end of your life on this Earth. Remember, *"Death is real;"* It happens, It has happened to me and those before me and therefore, it may happen to you and anyone in this World. You will never protest against it or fight it. You will never escape it – but you can overcome the challenges imposed on your life by the death. Life is by chance, but death is sure. Never blame death in this new journey of life of grief, pain and suffering; just wield courage because you can still make it in life – if you are determined.

Life is a journey with ups and downs, and every journey has its own challenges depending on the weather, terrain, environment and general situations surrounding the means and the nature of Transport we use – But if you are determined, no matter what, you will get to your destiny, which is

Preface

your greatest achievement in that Journey. Therefore, 'The Life Mania' is my story – by it 'I am defined and judged' – now you have the opportunity to know and understand me better.

THE MANIC SUNDAY EVENING

Death has got no favour; it comes to any person and family it chooses – at a particular time and we will never escape, nor protest against it. We are all (and will all) be victims of death at a chosen time; therefore, never worry or laugh – just prepare for your turn.

Life is a chance, We are not determiners in living this life; any second of the life we live, is full of chances; A chance to die or to live, a chance to gain or to lose; and a chance to love or to hate... Of course whatever we call chances, some are good and some are bad, some come and vanish quickly without being noticed, while some stay with you forever. These chances, whatsoever they are (either good or bad) extremely change your life to suit its moments. These moments of life can either be desirable or undesirable; but the way you handle life, is what changes your life to be either good or bad. When death takes its chance – it will be manic, but you are the only one to take that worst chance of death and make a better life and future. You have the power to make a better life and future despite the difficulties resulting from the loss of a loved one.

It was a Sunday evening in 1992 when all seemed to be like heaven on the earth as South Sudan's rebel controlled the small, but busy border town of Kaya. The Sudan People's Liberation Army/Movement (SPLA/M)'s main agenda was the promotion of the indigent cultures – Sundays in Kaya are special days for cultural fiesta – where different tribes gather on the showground for cultural salsa, which normally commences in afternoon hours. On that day, my Father, Mr. Martin F. Jacobs was not feeling well.

Being a cultural gala day, by 3p.m, everybody at home headed to the arena with the exception of my father, my Mother, and an aunt called Achi (wife to Arckangle Bashir, General Intelligence Security (GIS) officer of the SPLA/ M.

At 4p.m, my mother went to get a medical doctor to attend to my father. My father was left at home with Aunt Achi. A close family friend who was an officer of the Sudan People's Liberation Army Movement (SPLA/ M) came home. He found my dad alone in the house and injected him to death. The officer then went and reported himself to the Military Police Barrack that he had killed a person. Of course it was a taboo by then to run to the military barracks for protection whenever one found himself guilty of some crimes with the intention to avoid facing revenge by the victims or their family. When my mother got home, she was in disbelief to find her husband whom she left sitting, chatting and laughing some few minutes earlier, already dead and laying on the ground, as if somebody might have throttled him to death.

Achi came to get us from the gala. When she told us the sad news, we could not believe it. This could not be my father because he was healthy and could not just die that way. He never used to smoke, drink and was not even on drugs. It was impossible for a healthy person like him to die just like that. We dashed home and found that it was real. He was dead and it was a real manic Sunday evening for us. The entire situation was as if I was dreaming – something bad had happened and that was the death of my father. My father died and left us in the territory under the control of SPLA/ M, a territory where ordinary people only survived because of the grace of God.

The SPLA/ M claimed to be fighting to restore good governance and rule of law, respect for Human Rights, and Democracy; yet in its controlled areas which they called liberated areas – there was no rule of law, no respect for Human Rights, and no democracy but only terrorism of the local civilian populations by the SPLA/ M. This officer of SPLA/ M knew exactly what he had done. Unfortunately, the following day, he was freed, walking the streets of Kaya in his military uniform, while we were mourning. It was unbearable to see our father's killer walking freely. He has never come to pay homage to us as a family so as to try explaining to us what happened to this day (as I write this book). This made us somehow believe that, he simply avenged because of past odd experiences between our family, and his.

Of course, my father died and left us in the New Sudan of the SPLA/ M where you could kill, loot, rape and commit any kind of crimes as long as you were affiliated to SPLA/ M or your victims were from other tribes that were considered second class or had a person of high ranking in the SPLA/ M force. This person voluntarily reported himself to the authority because he knew he had committed a crime, but he was set free even before any investigation was done. He was declared not guilty without any forensic examination to determine the cause of the death of my father. Even as a family, we have never visited him, or called for any statement on the matter. It was a painful experience because we, the people of southern Sudan, took up arms to fight for our own freedom and happiness – which has its foundation on Human Rights, and desire to be free and enjoy rights that are alienable to all mankind.

We took up arms because we wanted to experience justice, but we were disappointed by our own movement. This very movement of ours, in our fight against the Governments in the North, became worse than the system that we were fighting against. In our fight against the odd system, we committed great atrocities against our own people which remains remarkable, unforgettable and unforgivable, – which has never been accounted for, by us as an institution and as individuals who are responsible for these crimes. As a result of these crimes, and of our failure to hold accountable the perpetrators, we are in lamentation and this is causing national unity and sense of belonging to our Nation almost impossible.

The cross violations of both individuals and collective rights in South Sudan by the SPLA/ M roared silently. These cross violations according to the Human Rights Watch Report of June, 1994, titled "Civilian Devastation; Abuses by All Parties in the War in Southern Sudan," included the exploitation of mineral and natural resources; the indiscriminative attack on civilian populated Government controlled areas; the unnecessary summary execution of people without proper jurisdiction and disappearing of people from the SPLA/ M prisons; torture and abuses of the people in the harsh conditions of the SPLA/ M prisons for long periods without due process; looting, stealing and destruction of the civilians' properties; intensive raping of women and under aged girls; kidnapping and adoption of girls and married/unmarried women as wives; adoption and forceful recruitment of school aged children; injustices, inhuman treatment and torture and continued unlawfully arrest and detention of people without a hearing, as well as denial of access to justice; creation of conditions that make the living standards of the people indecent; creation of unsafe living environment where people live in fear, and without security and protection; denial of freedom of speech, movement, expression, political opinion, association and peaceful assembly, privacy; and a semblance of slavery and servitudes through forceful labour.

These are crimes this rebel organisation silently committed while at the international level by then, yet were not recognised. Great attention was given to Khartoum Government which was considered as a terrorist regime because the regime masqueraded as Islam. No one focussed on the situations in the south under SPLA/M. As a result, hundreds of thousands of the South Sudanese indirectly and directly became victims of SPLA/M violence for two decades without international interventions. The cause of the misery and crime against humanity in the New Sudan of the SPLA/ SPLA/ M has its root cause in the training of the SPLA/ M forces. These forces are trained under unbearable conditions – they are underfed and denied medical treatment. Their training sites lack basic infrastructure such as buildings and they are made to build their own shelters without being provided with building materials.

Above all, they are instilled with a wrong doctrine and are made to take oaths when receiving arms - saying *"This gun is my mother, father, brother, sister, life and money"* and *"Even my mother, father, brother, sister, I will shoot – the direct translation is "Give him a bullet" – wadiu Talaga, in Arabic language"*. The actual context of the statement of the oath means something different but since most of the trainees are children and primitive people conscripted and deceived from the cattle camps and farms from the remotest areas of South Sudan, they take it anyway.

Here, not only did a functional Government not exist, but since some of those trainees have never even put on cloths before, and know not what a government and law is, they had no time for interpretation, so they took the statement as real as it was put. This resulted in the forceful use of the guns to rape, loot and massive killing of the innocent souls in their territories. The crime against humanity by the SPLA/ M force was so high thata local area chief had to write a letter of complaint to the local SPLA/ M area commander which said:

> "Our grain and cattle are yours - because you are our soldiers, but have the private parts of our women become also yours too?"
> Peter Adwok Nyaba, the Insider's View, the Politics of Liberation in South Sudan; January 1996

The SPLA/ M's liberated areas are hopeless territories with hopeless people. Although people struggle to survive, salvation depends on their creativity. To make the matter worse, even the so-called SPLA/ M soldiers and SPLA/ M politicians are people without hope and their life is full of hopelessness which made them be wild – with no respect for human rights and dignity and therefore, no more protection and security for ordinary citizens because everybody is hopeless and just trying to survive. Consequently, those in better positions of power and authority turned to use their available resources to survive at the expense of the poor and vulnerable citizens they came across. This was the situation and territory under the SPLA/ M where our father died and left us, as orphans.

Particularly, through the way my father had died; we were left in a great fear even to inquire from the man we believed had killed him, what really had happened and how he had died.

We occasionally do meet each other – but he always demonstrates unwillingness not only for a handshake, but even to talk and be together with me and this instills more fear within me and affects me more. Hence, whenever I see him, my heart beats faster and I begin to feel as if my heart was blasting. Suddenly I become very weak, and it takes several hours in order for me to regain strength.

In the New Sudan of the SPLA/ M by then, the situations could not allow you to seek justice even if there is a need for justice. So, for your own safety; you just had to accommodate every evil committed against you and pretend as if, all is well with your soul. This was the great secret to survive the persecution, torture and death – where killings and torture became the order of life in the society, where there was no Government of the People to guarantee safety for its citizens.

SPLA/ MSPLA/M was a total disappointment to many southerners and Sudanese at large. The source of the conflict in Sudan was either between north and south or west and North. The root causes are all centered on the poor policies of the Central Government in Khartoum – to realize and respect the individuals and collective rights of other ethnic groups in the Country. That also became the sole purpose as to why South Sudanese had been in civil war for decades, struggling for liberation and dignity – which are the foundation of human rights and democracy.

Regrettably, SPLA/ MA/ M never reflected it at all in its liberation struggle, it rather demonstrated to be criminal and without conscience for her people. Justice is the cause of any liberation struggle because it is what we all deserve as humans. Unfortunately, you cannot pursue this justice in that so-called New Sudan of the SPLA/ M and perhaps, never even existed in the SPLA/M. The situations became worse because even the International Community by then also forgot ordinary civilians in the SPLA/ M areas; it was only through God, that was how some survived death and torture by SPLA/ M rebel regime by then. Yes, my father is dead, I needed justice; yet, I didn't want to die too, because I valued my life and would wish to remain the heir as his only boy. Therefore, I had to forget about the entire matter of justice for my own safety.

"Safety is the first concern of the wise, but the fools are careless about their own safety because they do not know the value of their own life". Safety must be our primary concern – even though we know that one day, we will all die – but as for now, we need to live and contribute to this World till when our own appointed time comes for us to depart from this World, in death as ordained by the divine creator of humankind.

The death of a father is the worst experience of any child and leads to great pain and grief – but one thing you need to understand is that death is the end of mankind's earthly life. Shawn Michaels, the WWE Superstar, once said, *"Everything that has a beginning, has an end"*. Therefore, whether you are killed or you die a natural death, death is for you and you will never escape it in this World; You may struggle against death but at the very end of your struggle, you will still lose to it; for it is in death that your earthly life will cease. The death of my father was extremely painful just as death is always painful to anyone who experiences it. So we have to be prepared to face it because at the end of the day, we all have to experience it.

When we are prepared, accepting it becomes easier. We were not prepared for my father's death. So His death brought confusion into our lives because we didn't know what to do and how to survive without him. This is because of the way our father had trained us only as spenders and not finders and he is the only one that worked hard to get what we needed. This, on one hand was a great mistake because in cases of unfortunate situations as his death, those of us left behind suffered tremendously because we were not trained to find something by ourselves. When death happens, those that are left behind always suffer, especially if they are not naturally creative.

Death is not good because it brings suffering; death is a maniac because it has no favour for any person from the very beginning; if it comes to you, it will never reason whether you have people that depend on you and whether, when you die, those that depend on you are going to suffer or not. This is simply because death is a divine mechanism to accomplish the end mission of mankind and take us away from this World to the next World, as well as to separate us from each other temporarily till the day of resurrection; when we will all meet again.

However, our reunion with those who died before us depends on our individual relationship with God and how we spent our life on this earth.

However, because of the ultimate wickedness of mankind, death sometimes seems to bring to us a sense of rejection by God because if God is fair, loving, caring, merciful, gracious, why does He allow death to come to us? Naturally, when man is hit by danger and particularly death, man will try to reason with God.

Attempting to reason with God always brings human downfall– as a result, we automatically find ourselves somehow, sometimes in rejection of God. Reasoning with God on the basis of our daily problems is not a sin as long as our reasoning never leads us to commit sin against God Himself by driving us away from Him. God is not against any reasoning against Him – He created us to reason, but our reasons must not lead us to sin against Him because sin is what God is against.

The death of a father affects the child's moral, emotional, psychological as well physical world if there is no one to support and stand by them in their new life journey as orphans.

You may not want to experience it, but you may not also prevent it from happening to you; because it all happens unexpectedly by itself and its' chances, therefore, none can stop death on our ways, but only God when it pleases Him alone. However, grievances will never help you at all, or cursing God will never be a solution to your pain and suffering, and detesting those to have done that to you will not save you in your situation. Your salvation, when encountered with pains and grief is only courage and self-confidence. Courage is not the absence of pain or fear, but the ability to put up with situations and take positive actions and direction with confidence; while confidence is having positive knowledge of yourself, despising your wickedness and taking situations or challenges at hand, easily with trust in your inner being, and God alone.

Left alone
in the Journey of life

Our human relationship is a business for gaining from others, if they cannot profit from you, they will abscond you in your World of suffering. We are in a society where no one wants to take other people's burdens but they want theirs to be taken.

Mr. Martin was a respected and responsible member of his Community. He spent his career life working with, and for the community. Our home was everybody's home, and so were our meals. We shared all we had with others. I remember, at times in our boy's room, we could be more than five people sleeping together and sharing a blanket. I was still a child and all that I knew was that our family was a big family and my dad was from a very rich kinfolk. We had lots of uncles and aunts, cousins and nephews, in that family; everybody was our kindred and was warmly welcomed. My father had lots of friends from all walks of life, visiting us and none of them would ever pass by without greeting us. This was a real pleasure for us, as a family. This is the family I was born in, and enjoyed my status as a son, and was brought up to be loyal to others, to respect others, to love others and treat all elderly women as mother or grandma, elderly men as father or grandpa, young girls as sister and boys as brothers. That was the code I was brought up with.

The News of his death was a shock to everyone. Lots of people paid their last tribute to him during his burial and as a family, we were overwhelmed by the support we got from the local community. We knew our father was dead but he left lots of friends and relatives – whom we knew would be there for us to offer us the protection we needed because life in the SPLA/ SPLA/ M controlled areas was very difficult.

By then you could be raped, killed, beaten, tortured and your property could be looted and there would be no case against your proprietor because SPLA/ M knew nothing like justice and therefore, it was almost impossible to survive in such a situation without strong people to stand by as shields. After his death, we continued to receive visitors until the moment life became difficult. When we had less to survive on; people started to vanish without a trace. Some began to bypass us as people they didn't know before. Even the very colleagues of my father, and those uncles and aunts who we considered our kin by then, turned their backs on us, so we were left alone in that journey of suffering.

This turned into another big battle within me, because my father had been a very popular, very kind, and very loving and above all, an open-hearted and handed person. He never watched a person suffering as long as he could afford to do something to help. Our home was an open door home, everybody, known and unknown, was highly welcome. I really admired his life, and all I wanted was to be like him because everybody praised him during his funeral rites.

I was proud of his life. But this ambition came to a crossroad, I never wanted to be like him again; so kind, loving, open-hearted and open-handed, and popular because when he died, those he had been kind, loving, open-hearted and open-handed to, and his popularity of being good and a person of service to his community, became of no value. He was forgotten and his family left to suffer, without receiving any appreciation from the community and authorities for the good things he had done to others, and the community.

This brought a great battle within me, to be good or bad and the most serious one was the struggle to find the purpose of my life.

It was really a dangerous battle because I was struggling with who I really was and my personality.

The pain I went through almost wore me out: auspiciously, my struggle to know my identity because of the situations we had been through when father died – lent me into recognition of God's purpose for creating me as human in this universe, and to be more receptive to life with all its implications. Hence it came to be my creed that,

> "I am created in this universe to bring joy to others, to make others enjoy dignities and rights that are inalienable for all mankind and above all, to make life more meaningful to others".

This doctrine was the beginning of my change, my growth and positive directions in life, and to know that,

> "I do not live for man but for God and I will do to others what is required of me by God even if man may let me down, and disappoint me in every aspect of life in this World."

These creeds brought to an end, the great battle within me, and it became the rebirth of my original ambitions to be kind, loving and an open-hearted and open-handed person just as my father was.

This World and everything in it is fun, even our own life and relationship is great fun too. Human relationship is not for free nowadays, and therefore, behind any human relationship, there is a selfish interest that holds the relationship. Once the interest is satisfied or failed, definitely the relationship is over; and that was what happened with us, after the death of my father. Selfishness has turned us to disassociate with the poor in our society because we are afraid of responsibilities – as poor people in our contemporary greedy and selfish Society are associated with begging and considered to be a burden to the others.

However, as I had grown up; when I looked at a poor person and glanced at the rich person, I only see a person either physically fit or handicapped; the only difference is that the rich live expensive lifestyles while the poor totally depend on grace to live their life. This inspired me to ask people I ever came across, such questions as, "Why others are poor while others are rich?" Most responses were that; the rich are blessed by God; while others replied, that those who are rich are from well off backgrounds, while the poor are not. These answers became more confusing to me, but the truth still remains that, some of us are poor not because we are not blessed by God; or have never been to school or because our parents or grandparents failed to lay good economic foundations for us. Some people are poor while others are rich not because of the death of their parent(s), but because we missed collective intelligence, from our childhood life which now affected our lives in adulthood.

Therefore, those who are poor are not intelligent enough to make use of their acquired or natural intelligence for their own benefits like those who are rich in our society. A Poor person is not handicapped– a poor is like any other physical fit or handicapped rich person and can do something great to improve his or her life, but what poor people lack is collective intelligence. Poor people missed collective intelligence and therefore, in their situation, all they need is a redeemer to come to their world, to hold them by their hands and pull them on their feet through equipping and empowering them to develop their natural intelligence, just like the rich in our society

Sometimes we are poor simply because we lost hope and faith in ourselves due to the external life pressures that overpowered us and made us give up on real-life business, hence, only approaching life as it comes.

Yes, we were poor and left alone to face life with all its implications; and we could not make it all alone; no one ever succeeded on his or her own without backing, encouragement and support of others. We needed others just to encourage us because their encouragement to us was our strength to face life. This was exactly what Right Patrick Taban, formerly of the New Sudan Relief and Rehabilitation Commission (NSRRC)-the humanitarian wing of the SPLA/SPLA/ M, Mr. Archangelo Bashir of the GIS of the SPLA/SPLA/ M and Night Noel Byamunki became to us. Those people stood with us when our father died and never ever left us alone. They were always available for us either in social or financial needs. My success is not on my own account but because of them. They are my heroes.

The poor can still make it in life as long as they have people available to stand by, and with them in their sufferings – because by this, the hope they lost, can be restored. This was what those of Right, Bashir and Night did for us during my childhood, and even Faizel Badrodeen did for me when I first arrived in the Republic of South Africa as a refugee, which made me who I am to date. Of course, it is a very difficult task to carry other people's burdens. Therefore, even if we might be afraid to carry the burdens of others, we should never be afraid of them. We should never leave them alone because the more we come close to them, the more they become encouraged and strengthened; and this is the foremost help we can offer to them – to become successful in life.

Sometimes, we might have nothing to help in any situation and this nothing obviously is material to offer; on contrary to that, that so-called material is also nothing again because it is not a material that can strengthen and encourage a broken-hearted person. This does not mean that we don't have anything to offer in any crisis; we have plenty to offer because the greatest help that a person in crisis needs from us is our emotional support and encouragement, and the other things like material support will follow. We are all created with emotion which is the state of consciousness having to do with the arousal of feelings and awareness of physical sensation. However, our emotions are overruled by our fear of social responsibilities, and this fear is created by our egoism, and this made egoism is the worst enemy of our human relationship.

Egoism is what destroys relationships between us. It is also something that sometimes takes men away from God, as well as from recognition of God, the creator and sustainer of all. This makes Egoism as the major promoter of poverty and suffering in our contemporary societies. Egoism makes us want more and more, and therefore, nothing seems to be enough to us even if we are rich with millions of money while this may be more than what we really need. Egoism makes mankind unconcerned with other people's welfare and that is why, we are no longer concerned with the welfare of the people in our neighbourhood to the extent that, we have more but we can't note that we have got more. We don't even share or give away some of what we have, or no longer needs or uses, to others who might need, or use.

Sometimes we feel happy to throw what we no longer need or use to dustbins than to give to others who might need or use it. Our egoism is making us forget that any person in crisis needs us more in their lives than ever before. In fact, crisis presents opportunities for us to love, to appreciate, and to have mercy on others. A time of crisis is an opportunity to do good things to others that, we never got it before to do it. Thus, crisis time is a time in life where we all ought to re-examine our purpose of life and come to our own judgment whether we live as God created us to live for His Glory by taking care of His other creatures; or we just live as we want to live our lives.

Therefore, crisis era is the best epoch for us to look into ourselves, our attitudes toward the poor, or those in crisis and then examine our own individualistic interests in light of humanity. A time of crisis is a time for us to do to others the best of our bests, which we have never done before, this makes a time of crisis not only a time we should know ourselves if we are selfish or not, but also a time to extend God's love to others, as well as to allow ourselves to be vessels of blessing to other souls. We need to be good to others because our generosity is not only the medicine that heals those in crisis, but also the reason those in crisis praise God because of our deeds. Egoism is a weapon of people's destruction. There are lots of people in this world that are capable of great and to bring changes in our world, to restore peace and happiness that this world is lacking; but they are buried alive by suffering in our midst because of our egoism. We are there, but not concerned, we left others to suffer and could not offer our best to save and serve them.

We have got to love others; we have got to change in order to change this world because to change our World demands that we avoid facing back to those in suffering, but to face them and come nearer to them for their salvation.

MOTHER'S LOVE: THE STRENGTH OF HER CHILDREN

Mother's love for her children is stronger than any glue and is a remedy for a child's strength for success.

The death of a father is not only a bad experience for the children, but also to their mother. She is not only affected because somebody dear to her has already passed away and left a vacuum in her heart and life but also because she is left with a big responsibility, to take care of the children whom she was not prepared for alone in that hopeless war frayed State. She was left alone with a great responsibility to nurture us and bring us up to be responsible citizens of the World and be successful in life. With the death of our father, our mother was confronted with the choice to either fail or succeed in nurturing us to be responsible. She had to work hard and tirelessly to ensure that, we were not needy; she started to brew liquor for commerce to ensure that, we got the best life and living standard that would make us focus on education and the future.

Mothers are very important in the life of children and the success of any child depends on how much a mother offers to her child. This is measured in terms of emotional, moral, mental and physical support and encouragement of a mother to a child. When my father died, we had no hope for everything because we, in fact, underrated the capability of our mother to provide for us as our father did because she was a full-time housewife, without any trade, other than housework. We were worried because we didn't know the innate ability of our mother but she was indeed a great mum with great innermost being – which turned to be the foundation of our hope in life and success.

In that difficult situation of war and suffering, and being a fatherless child; the strength of our mother was our courage; her commitment was our hope; her courage was our pride and her pride was our happiness and above all, her happiness gave us peace of mind and joy; and this was how we made it in life during that time. A real mother will never leave her children alone no matter what the situation may be; because biologically, a mother is directly connected to a child than a father is to a child. The blood of the child is part of her own blood and what directly connected the two lives, a mother to a child is the Umbilical Cord, hence, the two are temporary, on physical sense separated at birth – but emotionally, a mother remains connected to her child till death.

The death of our father strengthened our relationship to our mother, and our love for her became stronger than ever before because she became the only person we had, and depended on. She took the place of our father in our hearts and our love for her was more than ever. As I write this Chapter, I was moved emotionally and reminisce her whereas nothing I could do or say because nothing is enough to appreciate her, nothing is enough to thank her, but this poem is all that I have to appreciate and thank all mothers in this World, and in the honour of my mother:

Oh mother, at first when I was inside you,
your womb was not a good place to be,
I kicked you and was just waiting for the time to come out in this World.
Unfortunately, once in this World,
it became a different story;
I could only wish I should have stayed longer

never to come out to this world,
To remain attached to you in the Womb
As I was those nine months.
Oh mother, is there any way or means
That I can return and attach myself again to your womb
    for the rest of my life?
Life inside you is better and good
than the life I have met outside.
Oh mother, I wish I could not grow up
to remain always under your arm,
where there is a shade from the sun,
and warm from the coldness of this World.
O mother, I traveled all over,
Searching for love, kindness, mercy, protection and peace
But I found none, in the world,

So, mother, you are unique from all
please mother, plead to your God today
to make me a child again
To return and remain with you,
in your arms all my life,
if not going back to your womb.

Mothers' love is the strength of every child – her love for me gave me the strength to do great things that I never thought I would have as an orphan and as poor as we were. Her love made me to think bigger and to work harder; above all, her love made me restructure myself and to manner myself to make her happy and proud. Her love was the foundation of my struggle, and if I am successful, it's because she remained not only with us but for us after the death of our father. Her big secret that made us be responsible in life was God. She knew that God is sovereign and can help, protect and guide us in every aspect of our lives in this World.

Therefore, before we went to sleep, she brought us together so close to her and prayed for, and with us; she was a Christian and always pointed at Heaven, and said, *"Trust in God, for He will never leave us"*. Sometimes when I misbehaved, she could call me and say, *"make me your mother happy, don't do this again because you will kill me, I will die of a heart attack, or sometimes she could say, your father is a good person, so why are you like this?"* It was a simple statement but very powerful, its influence was far-reaching in my life, since I loved her, I always had to make her happy and as my ambitions were to be like my father, I definitely had to live a responsible life and not to do things that would hurt and make her unhappy.

For her, anytime, was a time to talk, get advice and encouragement – she was a real mother with a real love for her fatherless children. The good thing about mother was that she never restricted us like our father; our father was sometimes very stringent, who could not allow us to travel long distance for holidays or get out to play and have some fun with other children if he was not sure of those we were getting along with. We were not allowed to do business or participate in any activity of income generation – because he was there to provide for us.

This was not the case with our mother. She left us free and independent; we were free to go for holidays out of the town, visit friends and go out to play with others, as well as involve in income-generating activities to earn our own money which she never used for herself and us. Whatsoever money we earned, we used it the way we wanted to use – but she was ever there to help us in making decisions on how we intended to use our own money.

With my mother, whenever I was going out from home; she had got three statements for me, *"be careful; behave yourself, and God be with you"*. Of course, when out there with friends, I was always very careful, I behaved and above all, God never left me alone, His grace and mercy has always been there for me till now. He has always protected me from the mouth of evils and death. I survived on several occasions – not because I did it myself to survive, but because the spirit of my mother is always there praying for me wherever I am.

Sometimes, the worst mistake parents make is to restrict their children from going out with other children. Children learn better from other children; when you send or allow your child to go out to play and have fun with other children, you are allowing your child to go to the school of life – to learn how to survive with others from different social backgrounds. It is out there in the school of life that they become exposed to collective intelligence which is vital for their own success in a lifetime. They learn lots of great things in life when they are out there with fellow children than when with parents at home; as a parent, you ought to know that, not all children are the same; and in their own world and groups, they are encountered with challenges in their daily life which they have to deal with, sometimes in secretive manners, whereas most of the parents are unaware about. When children are out there playing with other children, they are faced with decision making challenges almost every moment – the decision to follow others to do wrong things, and the decision not to; a decision to fight or not, so on and so forth. When children go out to play with other children, it is not only a play but a school of life where they learn, not from a blackboard and building class; but from life itself.

Outside there in the playground, for children, everything becomes practical, which is all about how to survive with others of different social backgrounds and cultures. Hence, they start to learn how to deal with complex people, and are exposed to networking and being connected with others, interpersonal skills and above all, how to protect and safeguard their values and interests without compromises. Something most parents don't know is that, when children are out there on their own as children, they become survivors – and everything for them there, are done as practical. They think for themselves, they decide for themselves, they protect themselves and they do things for themselves and this is the time they learn responsibilities – because they become responsible for themselves and everything that happens, thus, they learn to be accountable for their own lifestyles.

Hence, allowing your child to go out to play with other children is one of the three ingredients of learning which is "school of Life" where they learn from each other from playing ground on how to survive in this world. The second ingredient of learning through which they learn at home is from the parents, this coaches them the norms of living in the society; the third is the school where they learn from teachers in the classroom which only implants specific knowledge to them. These three species of learning are equally important for the success of any child in his or her adult life but the ones which primary are the two; that which they learnt at home on the norms of living in this society and, that which they learn from each other on how to survive in this World.

Children who are restricted from going out to play with other children out there become isolated in their adulthood and have difficulties in surviving with others. In most cases, they are rigid when interacting with any person of the society. They have poor interpersonal skills, poor connections and mostly, they are selective – they select people – those they select are possible people of high class or those in his or her own social class. They are very weak when encountered with challenges and mostly not a survivor – even if he or she might be highly educated; yet, they are rarely successful in societal life. They are often not happy and never enjoy their life and whatsoever they have, like others.

The Fake Society with Fake Purpose

The ideal to be rich has not only changed us but made us forget humanity; the poor in our society are suffering and remaining as farms for self enriches of individual elites.

Believe me or not; where there is a crisis; there – there is suffering; and where there is suffering; there - there is money to make from people. In today's world, man seems to be careless about the fellow mankind, for all man knows is money. This is exactly what the Chairman of Board of Directors of WWE, Mr. Vince McMahon said; *"I am a businessman, where there is a business, is where I am interested"* while the WWE Superstar Mr. Batista said, *"I am not in WWE for fun, but Money and whenever I see you fans, I never see fans but Money, money, money"*.

    This is a money-minded society, and the purpose of everything including our life is just money, to make money and be rich, nothing else man seems to be thinking of, than simply to make money. This made a fellow mankind's sufferings, pains and blood to be a source of money for others. We are in a unique society where the poor are becoming farms for the elites to accumulate wealth; a society where man becomes like an animal, surviving on fellow mankind. The common doctrine that reads in most people's hearts is to exploit and use others. Just exploit whoever you can, and make more money; use any person you can, and get on top with more money – this is a doctrine reading in the minds of most people, to exploit and use others; definitely wealth is the target, to be rich on others. Therefore, in case if you don't know, you better know it now that, we are in a modern society with modern business deals for making money.

Jonathan Erasmus is the right man who knew the secrets of this society; in his article titled *"Struggle is over"* which appeared on the Zululand Fever of 19th, March 2010. He said; *"Not everything, but everybody is for sale now"* What a senseless point? Many people may think he is just another crazy writer but is he? Maybe not at all; Yes, nowadays, man has become a big dealer; man is capable of making money on any person and this is a modern, the best and fastest-selling business worldwide.

In the past, People made money directly on others, just like this guy, Judas Iscariot made some few Denarii on Jesus by selling Him directly out to the authorities. This business of making money on others has always been there till the era of what was called "Slave Trade," but this is not the case now; People invented a modern business of making money on others, and that is, *"create suffering to people and make some money"* and if you can't afford to create suffering like politicians, then, *"just think big, grab the opportunity when people are suffering, create a comprehensive project or write a project proposal in their name, and make some money, we call it Charity or humanitarian services"*. Exactly, this is the modern world and society with modern business – for making money on fellow humans.

In South Sudan where there was a great humanitarian crisis and great suffering whereas people have no clothes, food, medications, water and place to sleep; business was flourishing. People are making money, others getting richer and richer; while others are becoming poorer and poorer. Though poverty was swallowing everybody everywhere, suffering becomes part of their daily life. No one cares. All that they care about is money; of course, money has become a habit of many in our society, and particularly with anything involving humans, and are "carried" for the welfare of mankind, it becomes all fakery because it is no longer for humanity, but money.

Fakery in South Sudan's humanitarian crisis starts with the New Sudan's idea of SPLA/ MSPLA/ M that was to demolish the old system of tyranny, discrimination, injustice, tribalism. The idea of New Sudan was to mop out poverty and bring social services to all people; as well as equalities and total freedom of people. But all these were just an idea because the realities remain that, the idea of New Sudan was just an illusion that remained without materializing. The SPLA/ MSPLA/M that came up with the idea of New Sudan, brought with them tyrants, discrimination, injustice, tribalism and absolutely redistribution of poverty and suffering than that in the old Sudan governed by the Arabs in Khartoum. New Sudan was full of new ideas that are too great to be believed. People throughout history are fond of generating great ideas. Mankind will always come up with farfetched ideas; however, for this idea to materialize, it is where a man will explicitly fail. Many people have an idea to get to heaven – but they may never get there because they don't know how to get there. Many people have ideas of making money and getting rich, but they may not make that money and get rich because they do not know how to make money and get rich. Many people fail to apply their great ideas into their real-life situations to make the ideas practical. Therefore if an idea remains just an idea and never materialized despite the fact that, we have all the possible means to make it materialize, our whole life is fakery.

We are not what we see ourselves in the brain or mind because of our very own brain and mind that generates the ideas is one person while our actions that materialize the ideas are somebody else. For this reason, our ideas can only be defined as fakery.

This was the situation SPLA/ MSPLA/ created by SPLA/ M with an ideal of New Sudan – where the idea neither reflects the people nor do the people reflect the Idea. The people of South Sudan with their SPLA/ M rebels seemed to be heading parallel to the Country's expectations and what they were fighting for by then. The New Sudan became just fakery, nothing good came out of it, and if there were changes by then, it was definitely from good to bad, and from bad to worse, as the lives of people never reflect the idea of New Sudan.

The Fake Society with Fake Purpose

Fake liberation organizations in South Sudan are common that have consequently founded the idea of New Sudan; every liberation organization has its foundation on the Universal Declaration of Human Rights to set common people free from injustice, oppression and poverty. The liberation struggle organizations' purposes are demonstrated by their love, protection and social justice to those they claim to have taken up arms to liberate. They, however, contradict their purpose since they end up committing atrocities against those they intend to liberate.

Liberation organizations should not be against any human race or religion and the motive of the liberation organization should be justice and equality, liberty and peace for all; in their struggle against powers and principalities of the regime of the status quo. Any authentic liberation organization is never against anybody or tribe or race, but against evils in them. Unfortunately, this was not the case with the liberation organization called SPLA/ M that existed in South Sudan by then; SPLA/ M committed great atrocities against those it claimed to be struggling to liberate; it turned its own guns on local people. The hallmark of the SPLA/ M is against a certain race. It was against the Arabs, it was against Nuers and definitely, against Equatorians. SPLA/ M forces saw any Arabs as traitors or enemies and they were not spared – to an extent that a Southerner born to an Arab was not spared.

In the 1991 leadership crisis in SPLA/ M, the Nuers were not spared by the SPLA/SPLA/ M and so were the Equatorians. All Nuers were taken as *"Nyiganti"*, traitors and any person associated with Nuer was put under surveillance. Definitely, it was against Muslims – any Muslims and the Black Southerners were considered to be like Arabs. On the other hand, Arabs were perceived as enemies; so, if you were categorized with Arabs, anything bad could happen to you in the SPLA/ MSPLA/M controlled areas. Instead of being liberators, SPLA/ MSPLA/ M became conquerors. Instead of democracy, it brought dictatorship. Instead of justice, it brought injustice and instead of equality, it brought discrimination and this was what we called the Liberation organization of South Sudan!

Today's liberation organizations are fake in their motives which is evident through their actions; they exist to liberate themselves, individual leaders of the organization, their families and tribes from poverty and to conquer others – which was not the ideal of any liberation organization during the colonial eras.

In situations where there is a fake liberation organization, there also comes Fake politics with fake Politicians and fake Governments; once an opportunity knocked ton my door. South Sudan SPLA/ M at that time, the SPLA/ M was headed to Tong Ayat Lual. Being an active member of this movement, the National Revolutionary Leadership Council (NRLC) asked me to act as the Deputy Chairman of the organization. "Ton this," I declined.

The Chairman and Commander – In – Chief asked me to be in the NRLC and offered me an acting position of Secretary for External Affairs. I again declined the position for reasons of my own belief that, 'I am not a Politician; In fact, I hate politics, and never ever wish to be a politician;' However, by default, I found myself always amongst politicians and talking politics simply because I am a patriot; – I love my country and my people; therefore, I will never keep quiet and do nothing as my people are being tortured, killed and are sufferings at the hands of fellow country mates. This does not mean that I am a politician, but simply a man who loves his country and people. Thus gives people a false impression that I love politics and that I live a political life.

My philosophy is based on the divine ordination. I believe God is the creator of all; He created mankind in His very image and made us all equal before Him. He ordained others to be farmers to work on the soil, to produce food to feed others; others to be teachers to educate others; others to be doctors to treat the sick; others to be lawyers to defend the course of justice for all, and above all; he ordained others to be politicians to bring societal order by making this world a second heaven and leading all mankind to live godly life on this earth. Politicians, therefore, live a sacrificial life to bring good governance and rule of law in our society as

God ordained in His blueprint. I believe Politics is a very vital segment of society and that it is the heart of the good things that happen in our society.

Those of us, who are not politicians, must not claim to be one but to play our active roles in our ordained professions to back up and support the politicians as they strive to bring good governance and rule of law which is the foundation of democracy, and the hallmark of human rights. A politician is a person who lives a sacrificial life for the cause of the entire community, and the welfare of his or her constituency is his or her first priority. Thus, politicians are very important people before God They are ordained by God to lead His people and rule His world as He wishes, but this is not the case with our society today. Humans go into politics with evil intentions – to rule for their own selfish benefits and to use taxpayers' funds and the natural resources of the nations for their own benefit.

Politics is an art of governing human society and politicians are the power behind this art – they determine the nature of the governance suitable for their people and put it into practice. It is sad that to date, politics has become a career that almost everybody is in the struggle to be a politician – while their own individual motives are egoism; their individual interests outweigh their national interests, thus most politicians are ready to sacrifice the nation and the entire citizens for the cause of their own individual selfish interests. This was exactly the situation in South Sudan during its two decades of civil war between the North and South, as well as post-war era. The South Sudanese's SPLA/ MSPLA/ M politicians and officers had no national interests, other than their personal individual interests. Most of the national revenue from the Oil production and Donor contribution for the reconstruction program in the South – are misused and deviated into the personal accounts of the individual SPLA/ MSPLA/M politicians and officers - leaving ordinary South Sudanese without access to social services.

The second reason I declined the offer of that key position was the motive behind asking me to take over the position. The reason was not based on the national consciences or capabilities but was associated with ethnic affiliations. I was offered that position simply because I am an Equatorian. The chairman and Commander in Chief General confessed it to me. For me, it was another practice of the dangerous politics of tribalism that South Sudan had been experiencing under SPLA/ MSPLA/M. Of course, as a nation, we did not have any honest politics that aimed to build our nation. What we knew as politics was simply propaganda by individual political leaders for their own individual selfish interests.

Thus, when any political leaders in South Sudan wanted to make a move, they first started with mobilizations of their individual tribal members and once they secured the support of their tribesmen, they would then try to manipulate the National political situations for their own individual interests in the form of national political crisis while using their tribes as tools. So my appointment was simply as a tool for securing support from Equatorians on beliefs that, since I am an Equatorian and being in that key position at the second powerful position, I would garner that influence to mobilize Equatorians to join the struggle against the SPLA/ M regime under the leadership of Salva Kirr and Riek Machar by then. I knew that and for that reason, I never wanted to be a tool to facilitate some one's selfish interests for power. Tribalism in South Sudan has a replica for fake national political leaderships which is the real enemy that is destroying South Sudan.

Tribalism has caused a lack of good leadership in the Country because it has buried some few qualitative leaders based on the fact that, they could either be from minority tribes or even minority clans from a particular tribe. Therefore, they could not surface because of the inferiority of their tribes or clans. Democracy and tribalism are not friends and will never be roofed together in any Nation. Therefore, where there is tribalism, democracy will be outfitted by tribalism. Due to this, the minorities will always suffer due to the fact that, in democracy, we believe that majority rules and where there is tribalism like in South Sudan, tribalism automatically works in the disguise of democracy – this means that large tribes will always rule the minority tribes. Thus, democracy is almost impossible in

Sudan and Africa at large even after fifty years of freedom from colonial powers because of tribalism. Consequently, Africa is faced with a series of conflicts because the minorities will never get their voice heard, or obtain their rights in a democratic manner other than through violence. Violence is used as a major tool to get both National and International attention to any political problems.

Of course, fake liberation organisation never only comes with fake politicians or fake government but also, *Fake Heroes*. Technically, a hero is a person who sacrifices himself for the sake of other people's salvation and well-being. In today's society, the idea of heroism is just relativism; it all depends on those who have helped us achieve our egoistic purpose. The Americans will call those marines who fought in Iraq war as heroes and the Israelites will call those who kill poor Palestinians as heroes – some call Sadam Hussein a hero and definitely Bin Laden was amongst those called heroes for the job done on 11 September 2001 and terrorism all over the world. But, are all those people real heroes?

How can a hero be a murderer who massacred innocent Palestines or Iraqis; how can a hero be a terrorist killing innocent people? And how can a hero be Dr. John Garang, the leader of the SPLA/ MSPLA/M? A murderer is not a hero, not even a person who inflicted sufferings on innocent souls. A hero is not a person who adopted and conscripted other people's children and sent them to be killed in the battlefield for his own selfish benefit while his own children were abroad schooling and living happy lives. More so, a hero is not a person with an ill motive or a dictator like John Garang. John Garang is never a hero because during his reign as the Chairman and Commander – In – Chief of the SPLA/SPLA/ M, not only many innocent people were killed by his troops, but also suffering was inflicted on many innocent souls in areas under his control. Under his leadership, many children were adopted and conscripted. They were sent to be massacred by the Sudan Armed Forces in the pretext of freedom, hence his heroism was because he served his own people through inflicting suffering, and death on others!

The fakery in our contemporary society not only ends in Politics but also permeates religions and fake Churches. The epoch of war and suffering is an era in which religion is tested if it is godly or not; it is a period where religion proves to the community whether it lives by what it preaches or not. Furthermore, it is time when the attitude of every religious person is tested and an individual proves who they really are. It is an era where the true color of every mankind is uncovered. The Suffering of the people of South Sudan during the era of North-South civil war was an era where religion proved that it is full of discriminations, hatred and above all, it is a business institution where people only don't make profits but, sly from others.

During the civil war between South and North, honestly, Religion demonstrates to be an institution where the really poor had no place to be served or helped without conditions. Religion became merely a place where if you don't know God before through getting into that particular religion, you will never know God again! As for them, God never existed outside the religion, but real sinners. The adherents have got a real knowledge of sin – yet they all, on a daily basis choose to sin.

In situations like that of South Sudan by then where suffering was inflicted on innocent souls, churches in the liberated areas of the SPLA/M were the only local institutions that seemed to be in a better position to help and serve people – because of the propaganda it used that, the Church was being persecuted by Islamic Regime in Khartoum. Because of such propaganda by the churches in South Sudan SPLA/ MSPLA/M controlled areas, there was generosity from their sister churches and church-related organizations worldwide for churches in Sudan.

However, when this generosity came to the Churches in Sudan, it became difficult for the real poor people to get it. Containers in Churchyards are full of relief aids; but if you don't belong to these particular denominations, you would not get any services. It then became no longer a matter of being a Christian, in order to get help from any of these Christian Churches, it was not a matter of being a Catholic, or Anglican; it was not a matter of being Seventh Day Adventist or Pentecostal or Methodist in order to get assistance from your denomination; but, a matter of whether you are known in your denomination!

If you were an Anglican and you get to Anglican Church, if you were known by the priest or Bishop, you would get assisted but if you were not known; then the question would be "Which diocese do you belong to?" You would definitely be referred to your diocese which you even wouldn't get there because it would be possibly hundreds of kilometres away and sometimes in the Government controlled areas. This means you would not get any help. I remember there was a time when there were relief aids in Adventist Church which were distributed only to their members, if you were not from that denomination, you wouldn't get help – and because of relief supplies as everybody is extremely poor and needy, people were just flowing from one church to another for relief aid. In South Sudan by then, relief aid became an instrument churches in liberated areas under SPLA/MM, used to bring people into their faith; as everybody was needy, people just jumped from denominations to denomination, not in search of God or true worship of God, but in search of relief assistance – in search of where to get basic assistance like clothes, Blankets, cooking items and food.

Religion by then was involved in a deadly business of buying people to believe in their God, buying people to come to worship God – because you needed to be helped, you would join the church and attend services with them from time to time so as to get assistance like clothes, blankets, etc. My mother was a very intelligent lady, she was and is an Anglican but because she also wanted us to get a share of those relief services, she started attending fellowships in Adventist and because of her intelligence we got the help that we would have never got from that denomination.

Religions with its relief programs made people be trickery; and in fact, where you put conditions for anything, while a person is in demand, they become clever and trickery; you automatically become foolish, and they get what they needed. The action of the religions by then in comparison to what it preached was totally parallel. Religion says, that there is only one

God and this God created all mankind in His very image and gave sun, rain and air to all mankind without discriminating; He saves, protects and provides mankind indiscriminately. It further preaches that you love your Neighbour as you love yourself. However, this very religion never lived by what it preached.

In fact, Religion loves wealth and money more than God – to an extent most religions seem to be ready to sacrifice God for Money, but not to sacrifice Money for God; the religious people looked to be ready to sacrifice their neighbours for their own personal gain, but not to sacrifice themselves for their neighbours. Religion is where love is simply a word but not an action; where the doctrine is simply beliefs but not the norm and it is where everybody is feigner. I am a religious person but I can confess that religion is an institution with no credibility to talk about God, and His Love for mankind. In fact, the contemporary religions are lost institutions; their practices are not only contrary to God's ordained practices but also contrary to the cultural values of any unreligious society because practices in the religion are just Satanic.

I remember when I first arrived in the Republic of South Africa; I visited the Government of the South Sudan (GoSS) principal Liaison Officer in Pretoria, Dr. John Yah Gai. It is there where I met a fifty-year white lady, an Irish citizen who had been a missionary in South Africa for about twenty years. She greeted me and after some minutes, she opened her handbag, pulled out a Christian Truck and passed it for me to read; I didn't want to embarrass her, so I took the truck and put it in my pocket. After brief introduction, we exchanged contacts and she told me she wanted to be a missionary in Sudan, this sounded interesting because every Christian Missionary wanted to go to Sudan by then to preach their gospel because they were made to believe that, Sudan is Islamic Nation and therefore, the souls in Sudan are desperate for their gospel.

I looked at her and then, asked her, "What good things do you have to offer to the suffering people in my Country?" She answered; Love, *"I just have to love them"*. I listened to her for a while and then departed in peace and after a few days, she called me and arranged for us to meet at Carlton Centre in Johannesburg by the Spur for some coffee. I went and met her; this time, she asked me an unusual question, "Mr. John, What do you think about sex outside marriage?" This was a complicated question I have ever been asked by a lady. So I decided to be intricate. I answered; "It all depends on the motivation of the Heart." This was the answer she never got from any person she had ever asked before me; the responses she had received before were usual – sex outside marriage is a sin or normal. I claimed to be a person who knew nothing in the Bible, she started preaching to me about God, Jesus and Love. She is a member of a very small Christian movement founded in 1968 in the United States of America by an American Jewish called David Brandt Berg who believed that sex is God's love and believers of God must show God's love to others and this might also involve sex, at times. She was so excited about my personal view on sex and her excitement influenced her to open up with me about her personal life history as a missionary and this religious movement – she belonged to.

She said that she used to stay with five African brothers at her home and all those brothers shared her and she ministers to each and every one of them every day *(of course, ministering to them means having sex with them every day)*. This was her ministry for brothers who were needy. She proceeded on, by saying that, "The best way to evangelize people is both to teach them from God's Word and at the same time giving them physical affections, (that means sex) whenever necessary". I picked an interest in her and was always in contact with her – my intention was all to know more about the religion and how they worshipped. In our third meeting after she had good knowledge of me, she asked if I could use one of my contacts to get her a visa to Sudan and arrange for her where to stay; I replied by saying, "If there is something good that you have for my Country, it will be my honour to do so." And then she said; "I love your people, I have been praying for your Country for twenty years. You people are so dark, tall and strong – your people are beautiful trees planted by God that has good shadow for one to be under it – I just wanted to get to your Country – to love your people" she continued,

"You know, your Country suffered so much from religious persecution, therefore, your country needs a true religion like our ministry, but not old fashioned church doctrine, - the Good thing I have for your people is Pure Love of God"

I paused in a deep breath, gave her a big smile and eye contact and said; *"Everyone is free to get to my country and so is, in hell."* Sex in this Christian movement is just an extension of God's love to each other; a married wife will agree with her husband, leave her husband alone and go to share God's love with somebody, and vice versa. They all just share each other and it is all in the name of God's love!

This Christian denomination has a very important document which is called *"charter"* which contains policies and set of rules that govern the movement of the members. Their positions on sex are according to Charter 273 which reads,

> Our communities do not prohibit sexual relations between a married person and someone other than his or her spouse, as long as all parties involved are in agreement. However, care is to be taken that such relationships do not affect the stability of their marriage that if such liberties are exercised, no participants or third parties should in any way be harmed or offended as a result

On the issue of homosexuality; Charter 306 reads

> Male-with-male sexual relationships are specifically forbidden and condemned by Scripture
> (Romans 1:27; Leviticus 18:22; Genesis 18:20-22; 19:1-29).
> We have therefore ruled that any male members found engaging in any such sexual activity will be excommunicated from our fellowship;

while on section 233 the charter reads,

> Scripture does not forbid female-with-female sexual affection, nor do we. However, strictly lesbian relationships are not permitted in our communities (306)."

They believed that the boundaries of expressing God's love to others could at times go beyond just showing kindness and doing good deeds to others. Even sex can be used as evidence for other people to express the Lord's love.

> If a brother or sister is naked and destitute of daily food, and one of you says to them, 'Depart in peace, be warmed and filled,' but you do not give them the things which are needed for the body, what does it profit?"

they quoted James 2:15-16 NKJV to support their beliefs and action for having sex with others in need for sexual intercourse.

The charter further reads;

> Teenagers are to be educated as to the responsibility of engaging in sexual interaction, and those 16 and 17 years of age must have the permission of their parents or resident guardians to engage in any sexual relations. Teenagers aged 14 and 15 may date others aged 14 through 17, but only with parental permission; No sexual interaction is permitted for those under the age of 14.

Today, there are many religious denominations just like this one in Christian circles – although they all use one Bible – yet they all differ in their dogmas and are opposed to each other because today's religion and churches are fake – their doctrines are not God's. This man-made doctrine which is fake doctrines has made our fake society with fake religions and churches which will never take mankind to Heaven, but direct to Hell with no compromise. This religious denomination is in Christian circle, they are Christians like other Christians – but is this godly? Is this doctrine of immoral sexual conduct ordained by God - that we should have sex with any person because this is the way we can express God's love for others? It is just another fake doctrine, fake religion and fake church;

I am not in support of Evolutionism, I am not fakery on my knowledge of the Bible; I was a biblical Student, I studied the bible for about three years from a good Bible College called Kampala Evangelical School of

Theology (KEST) in Uganda with highly qualified lecturers. I studied the Bible from the first verse of the first chapter of the first book in the Bible (Genesis) to the last verse of the last chapter of the last book in the Bible (Revelation); the more I studied the Bible, the more it became worthless to live by it, and the more it proved God to be fakery.

Where religion is becoming fakery, automatically comes *Fake Women and fake men with fake sex*, a real woman becoming a fake man having fake sex with fellow Women while real men becoming fake women by sex and having fake sex with fellow men; it is fake because it is not God's intended purpose. God's original two reasons for sexual relations were: *first*, to be the glue between a man and a woman which is to cement their relationship as a wife and a husband, and *second*, is the procreation work. But now, this is not the case, mankind turns everything upside down by forging their own system contrary to that of God – man can go with a man while a woman can go with a woman, and it is normal even if the practice is not as designed by the original creator.

This is a fake society where everything is becoming just fakery including Humanitarian services; in the war that affected South Sudan, the New Sudan Council of Churches (NSCC) received international donations such as Blankets and clothes which were supposed to be distributed to orphans and other vulnerable people in the rebel-controlled areas of South Sudan's town of Kaya and there was notice placed outside in the front of the office requesting for orphans, widows and People with Physical Disabilities to apply for this assistance. I was an orphan and decided to grab the opportunity too, my sister and I applied to the NSCC office for assistance, unfortunately, not only me and my sister but most other orphans and vulnerable people never got what was supposedly for them; we were later told that these items were finished and were told to wait for the next time.

How come these items finished while we had never seen any distribution taking place? Where had they gone?

And who were those that got these items? Indeed, these relief items were distributed but only to the elites and their kin, while the balance of these relief items was sold and the money went to the pockets of the individual elites for their sustainability. The poor remained suffering with nobody caring for them, as the elites only cared for themselves because of their egotism. Stealing in the name of the suffering people in South Sudan during the two decades North-South civil war became an aspect of authorities and humanitarian workers.

Kaya by then was the main humanitarian corridor used for supplying humanitarians' relief in the Country through Uganda and whenever relief convoy brought humanitarian supplies such as food and non-food items for the suffering people. After offloading these humanitarian items into local warehouses; some trucks would be reloaded again with some of these very items and taken to the SPLA/ M fighters in frontline, while a small percentage would be distributed to the local population mostly the families of the SPLA/ M officials and fighters and the rest, would be reloaded again in trucks and taken back, the same road it came from - to Uganda for sale, while people were still suffering. Humanitarian supplies by then never only met the needs of the poor but became a business of the elites. People were making money in the name of humanitarian services, while suffering continued on swallowing people in the country, and no one cared about them because everybody was very busy taking pictures, writing proposals and raising funds for his own benefit in the name of poor and suffering people in war ragged South Sudan. We are in a money-minded society. Everything a person now involves in, they will always convert it in terms of money – and carbon copy themselves to ensure they gain – even if others will suffer.

We are in a fake society with fake purpose; we carbon copy ourselves and our purposes in order to make money using our carbon copies and carbon purposes as politicians or humanitarian workers while our ambitions are totally selfish – to take advantage of the poor and suffering for our own egoism. Our society is corrupted with greed because of egotism and as a result, people are suffering everywhere while the sense of humanity is disappearing. Our selfish interests come first, then the welfare of others.

The sense of solidarity turns to be senseless – especially where there are no personal interests or something to gain. Our society today values money more than the soul of a person. It values wealth more than the welfare of a person. If there is anything that can give us money and make us wealthy in this World, we are definitely ready to sacrifice somebody's soul and life without delay. Because of egotism, the world is in problems; because of selfishness. We are in a big problem – as most of us have become farms where others harvest their wealth, and our existence is now only for selfish interests of others – to make them rich as we suffer and die in poverty. We are in a society where solidarity has no place, and everyone is for himself. We meet where we have our own individual interests and we depart where we also have our own individual interests. There is nothing now like common interests for humanity. We serve and save our interests but not others'.

Our purpose in everything sharpens the way we think, and act. So we cannot separate purpose from our life because our purpose demonstrates our innate and what we exist for. In a situation where you have developed egocentrism as your purpose, which is fakery by nature – your life becomes fakery too because you will focus more on what you as an individual will benefit and gain from any situation or any projects – without conscience of the impact of your actions on other people's life. The purpose of your existence should not solely for yourself, but for God and others. We exist for each other – for this purpose, each other is your immediate family, your wife or husband, children or parents, brothers or sisters, kin or friends and your community including everybody in the universe; they are there for you, and you are to be there for them. This means that the core purpose of all mankind is taking up social responsibility. Social responsibility is ideal of caring for each other, supporting and contributing positively to the cause of others' welfare – so that, they may enjoy these fundamental rights which are inalienable to them as any other humans, and this includes you. To care for each other means to be accountable for the purpose of your existence in this world – that is to clearly explain what you have done to others for the cause of their welfare and existence within your limits as responsible Universal Citizen. Fakery is our human insecurity; and in a situation where the society and its purpose is fakery, people suffer tremendously; fakery is crisis in itself – it is the strength of every humanitarian crisis – we helped as if we never helped; we donate as if we never donated; the more funds we received, the little fund we have for the project – completely nothing was, is and will be enough. Today, there are people suffering everywhere – this is because of the fakery of our societies and purposes as we are more of egoism; to gain more for ourselves then to offer for others' welfare.

Because of egotism and selfishness, we have reached to an extent of grabbing what belongs to the poor, for ourselves and letting them suffer, as we wait for another opportunity to grab again from them. Thus, grabbing what is for the poor becomes mankind's habits both as individual and corporate in our society today. Hence, where there is a humanitarian crisis, instead of using our knowledge to serve and save those in pain and suffering, we turn to use our knowledge to make benefits out of other people's sufferings by cunning resources from others in the name of the crisis. This is the fake society with fake purpose – the time for originality is gone and we are left only with fakery.

Many people in our society have remained hopeless with no savior or redeemer as poverty is consuming them while suffering weakens them and all we can see are fake saviors and redeemers struggling here and there to grab the opportunity to make more money on the poor and suffering people anywhere. Fakery is a social destructor hence our society will never be saved by fake people; but by honest individuals who are buried alive by the fakeries, of which their resurrection will mean salvation for all. Man, you got to think about others, you got to change to be original as God created you and stand for the purpose of your creation and existence in this world – to love and care for others' well-being. Selfishness will never take you anywhere than the simple grave where all that you accumulated will never get with you, but love will take you beyond the grave to another World.

STRUGGLE FOR SUCCESS

The way you handle your present life determines your future.
Life in itself is a struggle, to fail to struggle means surrendering to
failure in life.

My father was a breadwinner, and his death meant that we had no one to provide for our needs. His time had gone and ours had come so that we take care of our needs without stealing as stealing sometimes becomes a faster and easy means in our contemporary society to get what you need. To make the situation worse, he died and left us in a rebel-controlled areas where life was extremely hard, and there was no government or any mechanism to guarantee human security. It was a country where civil servants were volunteers and where there was no money, and even Bank, but only relief assistance that people depended on for survival. At least by the time he was alive, as a respected citizen, there was supply to us from authorities. These relief items that came in the name of the suffering civilians – which SPLA/M deviated for their military and commercial uses, at least never passed us without getting some rations. The elites always gave us so as we can sell some within Kaya or take to Uganda, and make some amount of money for buying other items not supplied by Relief Agencies. That was the system we found there, and we had to adapt to it, "get the relief items in big quantity and sell some out and live a happy life – while others are suffering." My father died when I was only eleven years old, and I knew things would never be easy again and as a matter of fact, what we used to get, we didn't get anymore because our mum could not afford to get them for us.

I know education is the only solution; I need to study hard and complete my school in order to get a nice job and live a better life again. But this is a future plan, it will take me several years in order to complete my studies – and even that hope is dim because, in the SPLA/ MSPLA/ M controlled areas, there are no proper education systems, not even one high institution of learning such as college or university. The rich send off their children to study in East Africa or somewhere as they can afford while the poor try in poorly conditioned local schools. By then if you managed to complete primary school successfully without being conscripted by SPLA/ M and sent to fight against the Regime forces in the frontline, consider yourself lucky. Being lucky means there is somebody to defend you from being conscripted or to release you when you are conscripted.

Schools by then did not actually serve the purpose of education but were organized institutions to facilitate gathering of small children to be entertained, and give some political orientation on the SPLA/ M ideologies which was all about instilling of deep hatred towards Arabs, until the age when those children were capable of carrying and shooting an AK 47. Then they were conscripted, offered some basic military training and were sent to the frontline while others were adopted as private bodyguards of the SPLA/ M officers. Those that were adopted as private bodyguards; some officers turned them as their house boys and were totally abused. They were turned to wash clothes and even some were forced to wash underwear of the wives of those officers. They were made to fetch water, firewood and were turned to be a watchman over the wives of those officers. They were ill-treated and sometimes beaten by the officers' wives. They were even denied food at home; in all these maltreatment, they could not complain against their officer or his wife or children or even leave.

When they left, they would be considered as deserters and would face punishment for deserting the national duties, which was imprisonment under abusive conditions, of which no one wished to get in it. When they complained, no one would listen to them and would only be called a disconcerted Red Army and sometimes even be punished. Though in that difficult situation, I still had a dream to be who I wanted be, not in the future but at the present time and the future will get me already who I am. Sometimes, the worst mistake one can make is to have a big dream for the future while forgetting that, the future that you are hoping and dreaming, starts with the present life. The idea of a successful future starts with the present life; investing fully in the present life – living the present life well – till the future gets you while you are happy and enjoying every aspect of this life without any wearies and suffering. So, I have to be extremely very careful with my present life and everything I do or think. With life, you don't have to wait for the future because the future never waits for those waiting for it. Life is a journey when you have got a journey for the next point; you have got to move in order to get there. If you stay, you won't also get where you want to get. If you want to have a good future, it is only your present life and struggle that will take you to that beautiful future you are dreaming of. This means that the future in itself, starts with the present and the present is the future. If you failed with the present life, consider yourself a failed person with the future life too; the future is not separable from the present; your present life is the core foundation of the future life.

Of course, for us in the New Sudan of SPLA/ M, there was no hope of completing schools and with the challenges to earn a living, I never gave up.

My hope and dreams remained higher and my struggle became greater. This made me be enthusiastic for success - in spite of all the challenges and lack of hope for many in the area. Life is full of struggles, but it is in the struggle that you understand life itself, and become rational in your actions. It is in the struggle that you develop a sense of intelligence and become responsible and successful. Struggle is the genesis of success. There is no life without struggle; no struggle without gain and definitely, no gain without a purpose. If only you need to be successful, then you must struggle. However, your struggle should be for something that is rewarding and gainful while your gains and rewards should be for a certain purpose. You don't have to struggle for something not gainful or rewarding by the end, and you don't have to gain anything without a certain purpose. You ought to live for a purpose. Whatsoever you live for, is what shapes your life, and describes who you are to the World.

A life without a purpose is a messed up life, it is a life with no sense of direction – it is simply an existing life – heading nowhere and not having knowledge of where it comes from. Therefore, it is a life without a goal, success, and nothing completely good in such a life. According to the English Webster's New World Dictionary' definition, *"Purpose is an object for which something exists or is done; it is an end in view of life or something, done not accidentally; exist by design."* Haplessly, many of us in this mania world are living our lives without a purpose, without even knowledge of whether life has a purpose or not. We just struggle and struggle to lack the actual knowledge of the purpose of the struggle – and as a result, we struggle, but we are never successful in life.

In order to know and find out what is the actual purpose of your struggle, you need to ask yourself a simple question, "What is the purpose of my life in this world and why do I exist, or why do I need to live?" Humans are very complex, sometimes with life; you can't distinguish the illiterate from the literate, the rich from the poor because all seem to be the same. They don't know the actual purpose of their lives in this world; they don't know why they need to live, and how they need to live their lives when they have the opportunity to live. It is true that, from the very existence of mankind, man proved to be more intelligent and nothing was, is and will ever be so hard and difficult for him than to simply live his life. To live life is where man has failed completely, and this is the author of every problem and suffering of mankind today. Lack of knowledge of the purpose of your life is what makes you to be reckless with your life, as well as to be simply misled in every aspect of life and struggle by your own individualistic misconception of life. Thus, your life lacks any genuine purpose which results in your struggle for moments. Because you do not have knowledge of the purpose of your life, you then start to struggle from moment to moment, till you depart this world in death. The reality about humans is that; the whole of human lives is a struggle - but most of the human struggles are only for moments and what contributes to a few percentages of the combined success. The purpose of life is now mania for mankind. This made man to be manic in life, and to struggle for moments only. When moments become the purpose of your life, then your future is deemed because the end of every moment of your life is suffering, hence you will never be successful in life.

I grew up in a manic society and each day of my life, I watched people very busy struggling for success, but what is it that they are busy struggling for? some struggle to find a wife or a husband – yet when they get married, they never get happiness but problems; some struggle to get children – yet those children they struggle to get, will never give them life; some struggle to get money, yet the money they struggle to get, is never enough and does not satisfy their egotism but what creates them insecurity and wearies. Some struggle for political leadership, yet the political position they struggle for, is temporary, it is what creates enmity for them and makes them have sleepless nights. Some struggle to steal and this is what lends them into prison and death. To make the matter of struggle so fun, some people still struggle to cheat on their lovers, but what profits them when they cheat? Nothing; some struggle to get boyfriends or girlfriends; yet the end is just jealousy, heartbreak and lack of peace of mind and freedom; some struggle to get work, yet the work they struggle to get never satisfies their wants and they don't find a solution to their problems. Humans are full of struggle; nevertheless, most of the human struggle is meaningless, it is only a struggle for moments and whatsoever humans struggle for, is not a solution to their problems and this becomes one of the reasons to fail to understand humans. We don't know our purpose of life – for this case, we struggle for what seems to be a life – while it is just a big moment and behind this moment, is another big suffering that we struggled to run away from. It is indeed so fun because a man will struggle to run away from present suffering, but will definitely run blindly into hidden suffering behind the new moment. This has become a reality that, most of us are blind.

We are blinded by the prospective moments, thus, we become one of the imprudent creatures under the sun – without knowledge of the purpose of our life, rather than the mere prospects of moments which we chase after, all our life. We run after moments that cannot take us to the very end of our life in this world and thereafter.

Of course, the death of my father made the situation to be very difficult for me, but I couldn't give a chance for the situation to take control of me; to give chance for a situation, simply means to allow the situation to take you into its own directions. Remember, all situations have no ends because its chains are strong, the present is like the future and the future is like past and the past is like the present, as time passes, you will find yourself in the same situation of life, with no change and progress, apart from being alive and possibly, in a good state of personal health. So I never gave any single chance for that difficult situation. At first, on weekends at the age of eleven years, I started to go to a Bicycle Repairer called Jeregu to help him in some simple work and by the end of the day, he gave me a hundred Sudanese' Pound and it was lots of money by then. My mother was my Bank, all my earnings, I saved with her and the money was hid in the Bible under the pillow of her bed. Later, since I have a lifetime plan after school, I decided to increase my weekly earning, so every day after school, I would go to his workshop, help him and my earnings increased from two hundred to four hundred and fifty Sudanese' pounds per week. Soon I found myself independent from my mom, I didn't have to ask any more for school material, clothes and any other things that I needed for myself.

I then saw other young people involved in Hawk of selling Roasted Nut, and I involved myself in that business – I used to roast the nuts and bring to the workshop for sale, and I gained lots of customers and there was lots of profit. I could remember, I used to buy nuts for fifty pounds, and when roasted. I would sell it for up to two hundred Pounds within a few hours. However, this business of roasted nuts was seasonal and I changed to going with friends in the neighbourhoods to fetch firewood from a distance of twenty Kilometres to sell during school holidays. As it is everybody's dream to be rich, own a business and be their own bosses, I left working in bicycles repairing workshop and opened my own workshop for shoe repairs within the workshop of Mr. Jeregu for a while and after some time, I moved away from his workshop and joined other friends in large workshop under a big Mango tree by Borehole on Kaya main Road. I worked hard, but money was not by then my purpose for hard-working and struggle, my purpose was education which is regarded universally as key to happiness - for all I longed was happiness; and was never driven crazy like other friends into smoking and drinking lifestyle – because I have got a purpose. The reason for my struggle and hard work was to gain money and the money I gain has its purpose, that was education because I know through education, I will be happy in the future. Purpose is what stretches motivation of a person to work hard and be tolerant – regardless of blocks or challenges in any struggle for success. Purpose is what allows a person to be determined, and take the right direction. My purpose for hard work and struggle was my salvation from destructive lifestyles most of my friends have fallen in.

In life, if you don't have a purpose for your hard work and struggle, then money will become the purpose of your hard workings and struggles, and when money becomes your purpose for any hard work and struggle – then your life is in mess. You will spend all the best of your lifetime working, doing sometimes the kind of jobs you don't even like – yet by the end of the day, the money you earned takes charge over you, and influences you to spend it all on worthless lifestyles that are not productive for your own future. You spend it on lifestyles that won't give you any happiness in the future. The money that was your purpose for hard work and struggle will finish after a few hours and it will never be enough, and you are left again with no or less money for your sustainability, and this is all the beginning of your failure in life, as well, the cause of your suffering. Money is not a good purpose for any work or struggle, but peace and happiness must be the purpose of your hard work and struggle.

The difference between me and my childhood friends was the purpose of our hard work and struggle, they worked and struggled hard only for money while I worked and struggled hard for happiness and this gives distinction in our lifestyles even as we do all things together in a group as a team. Money takes charge over them; when they get money they become crazy, throwing parties, drinks and women and for them, it was real life but when that money finishes, their life also stops, everything becomes hard again and they have to work and struggle hard again to earn other money and spend it in this same manner. Of course, drinking, having party or going to clubs and having many girlfriends is not bad because it is happiness in itself and we all need to be happy – but some of this happiness that lasts for only one moment of hours and the other moment of hours is suffering, it is not happiness but already suffering in itself.

If there is a life that can make you happy right now and later make you suffer, then that is not life and it is better not to choose such a brand of life because the end of it is just suffering.

Everybody is against suffering, no one wants to suffer. Unfortunately, most of us sometimes search for suffering on our own by choosing lifestyles that will lead us at the end in suffering. We intend to go for moments of happiness, than the real happiness. Moment of happiness is short term happiness that you experience for a particular moment while whatsoever comes after is not of concern to you that moment, only when that moment is over, then you start to experience worries and sufferings. Moments of happiness are not happiness by themselves but suffering because after that moment, there is no more happiness, but suffering.

In life, never go after moments but the real matter itself. Moments last for a while, moments will always vanish away and you will never get it again, but the real matter will last forever with you; I was never after moments of happiness but after happiness itself. This guided my lifestyle, and in all my struggle and hardworking, happiness was my purpose and I was determined that one day, INSHALLAH, I will be happy both in this World and the World to come with ALLAH in Heaven. Nevertheless, in any struggle, there is one real limitation, and that is your status in the community. Sometimes your own, or your family status as poor or rich, illiterate or literate in your community will be your limitation; that is to say, I can't do this because my family is this; I can't do this, because I am this.

Once you come up with this mentality of status, you will be limited to do certainties, and this will be sometimes extremely dangerous for your own success.

In fact, how others call us or consider us in that part of a community, and also the way we view our status in that community can affect us mentally - which can either be dangerous or good for our own success. They called and regarded me an orphan, they said the father of this boy was this and he is now this; it is for them that I am an orphan but as a matter of fact, in whatsoever challenges I encountered in life; I never considered myself as an orphan by then - because an orphan is simply an absence of excellent state of mind, that affects your entire being. The death of my biological father is only his physical absence from me in the present sense, to offer me emotional counselling and encouragement as well as affections that a child expects from a father. His absence in person for me does not make me an orphan – simply because I can do what other children with fathers can either do or not capable of doing.

To see yourself as an orphan because one or both of your parents are dead will only limit your abilities for success and make you more vulnerable in life. Throughout the situation we have been in when our father died, I looked at myself as an able child without a father who can achieve what other children with fathers can, or cannot achieve in life because in real life as a child I don't need either a father or a mother in order to be successful when I am out there playing a game with other children – because whether my parents are alive or dead, I will have to play the game by myself alone.

The death of my father never made me a handicap, I have my two legs, hands, eyes, ears like any other children at my age in school and in neighbourhoods and therefore, even if they have their father, they are not especial than me because I am very fit to do any work and think creatively.

I was really proud of myself because either it was at school or in business, or even in games during playing, I was the best or ahead of some of those children with fathers, and this instilled self-confidence in me that, even without a father, none of the children with their parents alive was as special as I was. To be the best you want to never require you to have your parents alive; you have to struggle for yourself alone, it is not your father or mother that examines you in school in order for you to pass. In the examination room, you are left alone as an orphan only with teachers and fellow schoolmates who might not be next of kin to you, but they become part of you in your educational journey. Therefore, it is your own struggle that makes you be the best you want to be in life. Whether you have parents or they are dead, to be successful in life, it is not them to struggle for you but to struggle for yourself. Your parents only play their role of offering emotional support, encouragement as well as affections to make you strong as you give your best in your strive for success. Success in itself is not the absence of failure, but an ability to learn to improve and adopt new strategies and methods of doing things better to reach your goals in life, in spite of the challenges. There is no success without failure; failures are stages in struggle and life that points directly to your ultimate weakness as a person.

Failures are stages in the struggle of life that aids you to improve on yourself and develop a new strategy for achievement of your personal goals. Failure was part of my life especially when I was with Sheikh Ahmed; I failed not because I don't have capacity or ability to do some of these difficult tasks, but because my own strategies are very poor and my inner being is so weakened; the fact is that you might be capable of doing something, but if you don't work on some of the weaknesses of your inner being, failure will always be there for you.

One of my greatest failures by then was a failure to smuggle a huge amount of American Dollars that belonged to Sheikh Ahmed for implementing his projects in a designed destination in another Country. Of course, this is an illegal project – everything is illegal. I had to get in that country illegally with this entire huge amount, support the team who were also illegal in that country and to leave the country again illegally. I had no single document with me. There in the Country, I was arrested, and the money was confiscated and I was detained for a while, of course, a country where people are poor – American Dollar is a life for them – when they see a dollar, they see salvation. Those officers took all the money and they could not take the case further because they needed the money for themselves – there, I was out and back to where I came from. It was through my failure to smuggle Money from one country to the next Country that I discovered my weakness. I was able to learn new ways and improved on my inner being to be smart, creative and then be successful next time. Failure is not the end of life and so it is not the end of struggling too, in this World.

Failure does not kill and there is always success after failure if this is the doctrine you believe in, – therefore, you don't have to give up with struggle and life when you fail - because you can still make it better and reach your dream if you continue with your ambitions.

Secrets of Success

Success is not only determination and acting on your desired goals but also discovering of secrets of life and living on this Earth before you die

In my struggle for a better life and future, I then realized that, People don't succeed in life because they are not capable, or they don't have potentials. All humans are capable and have the potential to succeed – but they fail because they don't have the real knowledge of themselves and never unveiled the secrets of life and living to influence their success. These secrets of life and living are what I term "the secrets of success" because without discovering them, your life is meaningless, you might work hard but by the end, you lose for failure and end up in suffering, and these secrets of success are:-

Being original; you don't have to claim to be what you are not. Don't pretend who you are not because that is to deceive yourself. Don't allow yourself to be led to failure by who you claim to be, while you are not. If you are poor, don't claim to be rich because by forging richness simply means you have to compete with rich people, dress like them, eat like them and live like them and as poor as you are, you will find all the little you earn, you spend on expensive lifestyle – leaving you with nothing in hands for future, but only struggle and suffering till you die because you are attempting to counterfeit who you are.

In my struggle for success, by default, I became part of a group of Mafias because my best friend, mentor and a person who took me as his own son, Sheikh Ahmed who is a Somali by nationality was a mafia and I used to help him with all his paperwork, managing his illegal projects and as a son, I took overall responsibility to ensure his projects were successful. Just as Nigerians say, *"like father, like son"*– I found myself automatically a mafia. I was in the forefront defending and protecting him; our relationship dragged me deeply as part of his group because he really needed my skills and services for his own success and I too took him as a father – I respected him so much – for respect to others, Royal to elders and protection of my dignity, is my core value. I respected him and all his members so much. I was loyal to him and his projects – yet, I had to protect my dignity and never had to compromise my decorum with any evil acts.

Sheikh Ahmed never drank nor smoked. He did not even shake hands with women apart from his wives; he lived a simple life of Islam, he was an ordinary person with an extraordinary brain. He was a real human but a real lion that never feared any person under the sun, except God only; whom he offered prayers to, Five times a day. But, those surrounding him, were in another World in that World of Mafias. Their lives were so different and evil was all that was in their minds and crimes were part of their daily lives. Those were the people, I walked with for miles in missions, shared a room and plate of food with, but I never followed them in their evil activities. I did this because I was more concerned with my future life both in this world and after this World when I die. My concerns with my future life both in this world and after this world when I die, became my safety from going to prisons, my safety from being killed, and a guarantee for my success in that life.

In life, sometimes by default, you will find yourself amongst the wrong companies – to be in the company of wrong groups does not justify you to be wrong or criminal as long as you are original to yourself, and never forged to live like them and do what they do. Being original to yourself require discovering your identity, who you really are. The big problem is that, in this world, some people don't actually know themselves and who really they are - all that they know is, I am Human, I have life and therefore, this is me. As a result of a lack of knowledge of themselves, when they find themselves in the company of wrong people, they are swept by their lifestyles and explicitly, they start to live, and get involved with criminals like them– which is dangerous lifestyles for any sensible person.

In life, there are struggles and in any struggle, there are failures and success; with your own life, you can choose to struggle or not, and with your own struggle, you can choose success or failure and this is the greatest choices you have to make in life, and act on them accordingly, whether you are by default in company of wrong people or not. All individuals own their life and future, you can choose your lifestyles and the choice of the lifestyle you make, no one forced you or put you in it. It is totally voluntary – sometimes when we are suffering, we choose it by the choice of our lifestyles - which in turn leads us to this particular situation. Of course, there is no doubt that sometimes our friends or other people, including the situations we are in, will attempt to influence us to a particular lifestyles that are either good or bad, but it does not mean that you are forced because you still have a chance to make a choice to respond to this particular influence on you.

This choice could either be a positive or negative response to the influence and therefore, your choice, determines your failure and success in life and struggle as general. The same choice determines your future life and destination and because of our own choices; we in one way or the other, become the very victims of our own choices. Sometimes we struggle in pursuing a moment of happiness, and joy by going to clubs to have some drinks, or joining up gangsters, and doing genus of things that gives us moments that we pursue and when that moment is over, our joy and happiness is over too – there comes another suffering – perhaps slightly worse than before.

Sometimes people go for the magic to gain wealth and this is most amongst the entrepreneurs. Sadly they are demanded by the magic to offer souls of their dearly one, in return. This could be your father, brother, sister, mother, children, wife or husband – since the idea is all about being a wealthy person – they have to do it and gain the wealth and be rich. The worst thing is that the wealth or riches gained from magic are completely for a moment – it is a temporary wealth and riches. It is a contract between you the prospective entrepreneur and the magic and anything that is contractual expires and when it does, the deal is over.

Of course, those who entered into a contract with magic gained a great moment of wealth and riches and after sometimes when they don't follow the rituals – something worse happens – they either die or run mad, and then their business collapses. It is what I call triple loses; first you lose your people, father or mother, brother or sister, wife and children to magic for a moment; second, you lose the moment itself and the third is that, you lose your life again to the magic and if this is the case, so what profit is it now?

Why go for such a moment when the ultimate end is losing all to magic? Life is an investment – the way in which you live your life, whatsoever you do as an individual and collectively must be an investment that, by the end, you profit. In fact, if anything seems to be worth for life in a moment and afterward, it will cost you; it is not worthy to do it; it is not worth a life because there is no profit but only loses. You got to be original to yourself in everything you do and think. In the midst of the wrong company, you still have the chance, to choose to be original of yourselves or carbon copy yourself like them and fail in life.

In 2005, I got a contract with a Swedish International Humanitarian organization operation in South Sudan called "International Aid Services – (IAS)' to enforce its implementing partners in the implementation of its' ECHO Funded "Jonglei Water and Community Development Project". Of course, I was domiciled in Uganda and had to travel from Uganda to Kenya, and then fly to the operation side in South Sudan. One weekend, I went for a meeting with the local community leadership in one of the small village about fifteen kilometres away from Pibor Town to enlighten them about the importance of their participation in the project activities as well as to spearhead in the sustainability of the available water points and other project outputs. I was accompanied by the leader of the local women group in Pibor by the name Mary. The meeting was held under a big tree in the centre, next to the house of the local respected elder in his late forties. This elder at the end stood up and said; my son, it is very good that your organization drilled for us water and now, we can no longer drink from the same water in the stream with our cattle; however, you have to know that, our problem is not just water, health and education.

> "We the people of Pibor (Murle) have got a big problem – that is famine, we and our children are starving; we have no clothes and as you can see, we are wearing nothing – we need food aid and clothes."

Yes, this was a very poor community and suffering was part of their lifestyle. But, their suffering was mostly man-made and sometimes caused by their own individual ignorance. This elder was a very rich person in that particular community with over one hundred cattle and a good number of goats. He was, however, naked as he was born from his mother's womb – with exceptions that, he had beads on his neck and putting one Sandal made out of vehicle wheel. He had got no proper house, sleeping on animal skins and at his home, there was famine, in his face, you could see poverty, suffering and weary - the children had no clothes and all seemed to be unhealthy and underfed.

It was my first time to meet him and I picked interest in him; I promised him that, the following weekend, I would pay him a visit. Exactly as I had promised, the following weekend, I got some washing soaps and food parcels and paid him a visit. This time, I was prepared to talk to him something about himself – of course, this was not what I was charged by my employer, it was my personal initiative to help him to know who really he was. We started a conversation and then I asked him; how many cattle to you have? He said, "*My son, I am a very poor old man and the cattle I have are a hundred and fifty*". I smiled and asked him, what are all these cattle for? One hundred and fifty are too many. He said, "*They are to be paid as a dowry when my two boys want to get married, and if I have problems, I will sell some out to solve these problems. You know that I am very poor and all I have are these cattle and goats*".

We had a conversation for about two hours and throughout our conversation, I was leading him to know himself very well, in particular, to know how rich he was and that, he could improve on his living conditions even without relief aid from IAS or any other humanitarian organization operating in the area as he was expecting. I left him and after three days, he came to the Compound where I was staying and said to me politely, *"You know my son, it is very good to go to school."* "Why?" I asked him. He replied, *"You are just a child but you know what I don't know... I was just stupid; that is why I am suffering and now I am planning to go to Juba and sell some of my cattle in order to buy clothes for myself, wives and children, and then to start a business"*. I appreciated him very much and wished him good luck. Lack of knowledge is a course of suffering to many people in our neighbourhoods and therefore, to be successful, you need to know yourself very well and to be original. If you know yourself and are original to yourself, you won't allow yourself to be dragged into suffering and poor living condition that will definitely affect your health and life while you have got resources to make you happy. To be original to yourself means to know who you are, this includes your available resources and how to use these resources in your disposal and your own life and live happily.

Sometimes people suffer not because they have no means to help themselves but because they don't have knowledge of how to spend their life as well as their own available resources. To have knowledge of yourself requires you to know and understand the meaning of success and the purpose of life. Success is not measured in terms of numbers of what you have or what you achieved, but it is measured in terms of happiness. People who are not original to themselves, in most cases fail to have the knowledge of themselves. They are not capable of using their life and their own available resources to live happy lifestyles.

Teamwork, as opposed to individualism; To be successful requires that you find your right team. This is the team that shares your vision and you have the same spirit and determinations. In struggle and life, you need others to be part of you, to inspire you to achieve your dream. It is through a team that you develop new skills and learn new ideas that on your own, you would not be able. Life is like a game, a good striker needs to find the right team and play as a team in order to be successful. The striker will never score against the opponent team if he is left to play the game alone against the opponent team in the field. The best striker still depends on the support of his team in order to score. He needs to have a connection with his teammates in the field, to pass for him the ball and back him up. The team is very important for your own success. Thus, if you need to be a successful soccer player, then join the soccer team because it is the right team that shares the same vision and spirit with you, but if you join a wrestling club, you will fail because you will never reach your dream of being a successful soccer player. Again, you will not be a successful wrestler because you are there by mistake, and it is not your dream to be a wrestler.

With success, there is nothing as individualistic; even the most successful person on this Earth, still depends on the emotional, material, social, spiritual and physical support of others. Therefore, to gain those forms of support means being collaborative with others.

This was a priceless secret that I discovered. I had to close my own shoe repairs workshop and join a group to open a big workshop that brought about my success in business by then. I was successful by then because through my team, I learnt from each and every member. I even learned from the most dualist member of the team because all mankind is created with very unique gifts. The team is what builds you up and makes you successful, especially if you join the right team. It is also what will destroy you and make you fail if you are in the wrong team. Remember, there is no success in independence and no one is too great enough to be successful without any assistance from other(s). Even the Greatest God, who is omniscient, omnipresent and omnipotent – still worked through and with His creatures. He worked with ordinary men like Prophet Moses, Noah, Abraham and Mohammed. He depends on His angels, as per the two religious books-"Quran and Bible". - In fact, God worked in a team, and for a man to be successful, he needs to be in a team. Work in a team, rather than working as an individual.

Individualism isolates us from collective intelligence which aids an individual to progress mentally and spiritually and materially. Individualism is what brings deadlocks to our reasoning capacity which leads us to the lack of creative thinking. Individualism also isolates us from God – because God is not interested in an individualistic person – He never uses an individualistic person. When God gives us a gift, He intends it for the benefit of our community. If you try to be individualistic, these gifts will disappear. They will die within you, and you become another dead living person because you will never be successful again.

Successful life comes from teamwork. We were born out of a team (a team of two people - your father and mother). We grow up in a team and live in a team. This team can be our family, our community, our friends and our workmates in the workplace. A successful team player – is a successful person in life because life is all about teaming up. We all hate to be alone. Life would be miserable supposing you were left alone in an entire city like Juba – with no one to talk to - you would just hate yourself and perhaps commit suicide.

When I read the biography of South African's International Icon, Grandpa, Nelson Mandela, I discovered that his success was not on his own - he was a very good team player and throughout his childhood right to his political career – he was connected with people, walked, worked and lived in a team. At the age of five, he was already a herds-boy. He looked after their cattle with other fellow boys and after the death of his father, he and his cousin Justice became the best teammates when he was adopted by his uncle. They rode horses and ploughed fields together and when his uncle decided for them to marry, both guys refused as a team. They decided to steal his uncle's best two oxen, sold them out and used the money to travel to Johannesburg. He remained connected to people and there, he met people like Walter Sisulu and his old university friend Oliver Tambo and as a group, they formed ANC youth league. Apart from that, Mandela and his friend Oliver Tambo decided to open up a law firm in Johannesburg.

Team is all about connections; it is what keeps us connected with others and facilitates our success. A team player is a person well connected and his or her connection with others exposes him or her for better opportunities and, makes him or her successful.

Grandpa Nelson Mandela was well connected. In Johannesburg, he has a connection with Walter Sisulu of ANC based in Soweto. Through Sisulu, Nelson became connected to ANC and it was his connection which made him be who he was before his demise (and even after that) – the highly respected person internationally. Life is all about connecting with others. To be a successful businessperson, you need to be connected with suppliers and customers. Connection is a very vital aspect of success and this is a team in itself.

The purpose of a team is not to gain an advantage over others. It is not to use others for your own selfish benefit – but it is all about learning together, being of help and inspiration to others as others might be to you. Therefore, together through learning, serving and inspiring; you will be equipped, empowered and motivated to give your best and to become the best you can be – which is success. Another advantage of team for your success is that a team helps you to know yourself better. Most of us don't know ourselves well. This is the greatest challenge towards our own individual success. Yes, you aim to be successful and are struggling for success - but how can you be successful if you still don't know who exactly you are? To be successful, you have to know yourself and your potential very well. This is the foremost condition for success. If you don't know your potential, you will always undermine your capabilities and will be afraid of doing what you are capable of, which will lead you into the first step of failure.

People who don't know themselves often make decisions that are opposite to their potential. In life, the consequence of any decision that is contrary to your potential is trouble and failure.

It is a team that helps you to know yourself well. It is through a team that you start discovering yourself – knowing yourself better about who you really are. For example, you won't know that you are gluttonous, until when you are in a team and there is a meal before you. Therefore, it is a team that helps you to re-discover yourself and know your inner self better. This is then what makes you start acting positively in a direction towards your potential which is the road to success.

Flexibility; according to English Webster's New World Dictionary's definition, *"flexibility is an ability to bend without breaking; Tractable, adjustable to change; capable of modification; not being stiff or rigid; easily bent"*; Flexibility is a point in a life at which a person pauses for adjustment and then engages fully to new changes caused by external circumstances – in his life or in the society, at work, and within environments, etc. – without losing his original purpose and vision of life. Flexibility is hidden importunate in itself for your success – it helps you to be more receptive and involved with whole aspects of your individual life and to travel safely along your journey to success despite the thwarts from life and its surroundings. In life, you don't have to be stiff or rigid. If you are, then you will fail because you won't be able to survive in this complex world. If everybody is flexible, we can bend in order to enter through a short gate without breaking into pieces. Therefore, if you don't want to break down in life, you have to be flexible.

Flexibility is core for any success; to be flexible is to acknowledge that, in life, there is a time for everything. When the time comes for particular aspects of life, you have to be receptive and adjustable to fit and survive in and through it.

There is a Burundian barber who is a friend of mine in the South African town of Empangeni. One morning, as we were talking about the challenges of life; he said, "in this world, *never force life.*" this was a very interesting statement and it attracted my attention because it was the time I already began writing the manuscript of this book. I then asked him, "Why?" He replied, *"You will get lost"*. The fact is that people who are not flexible in life always attempt to force things out; as a result, they always get lost and they end up blaming situations or others for their own failures and messes. To be flexible does not mean being weak in a particular aspect of life and its challenges. It is not bad, and will not cause a delay in reaching your life dreams. It is just a time where you position yourself in order not to be wounded by the challenges.

If you are not flexible in life, you will always make serious mistakes that may sometimes cost your own future, as well as that of other people – especially in the case of a group. This happened to us in one of the dangerous missions to which, I was in charge. We were sixty people traveling to a certain country through a country that none of us had ever been before. We were accompanied by five people we got from the boarder who to help us cross the country illegally to our final destination.

Of course, anything illegal means that there will always be a game to play between law enforcers and lawbreakers. We were prepared for anything, We crossed the border at night hours on foot for a distance of fifteen kilometres to board a truck hired to take us throughout that night to the next border; as a person charged with the responsibility of the group, I decided to be the last so that I never lose any person in that thick bush. We walked from mountains to mountains, valleys to valleys and rivers to rivers on that heavy storming night which was very dark and we were using a very narrow path. Somewhere in the middle as we walked in one row, the row was split into two - the first row with forty people and five helpers took another direction and we were left twenty and completely lost. We walked for eight hours non-stop till 6 a.m. When everybody stood, I went ahead to find out what the matter was. To my amazement, I found the rest of the people were not there! So, we only remained twenty people – of which nineteen were Somalis who could not speak either English or Arabic apart from their own Somali Language which I could not speak, and my interpreter had already gone ahead. Communication became very difficult; I had got communication equipment but the battery was completely off – I could not communicate all through. Of course, for our own safety, we could not walk during day hours. We, therefore, got into a thick valley to rest till night hours. We then tried to return where we had come from.

However, by noon, a group of ten people defected from us and we couldn't know where they had gone. Later by 4 p.m another group of eight people decided to leave – I remained with only two people by 7 p.m when we commenced our trip and tried to find our way back.

We walked through bushes – off paths and on paths till we came on top of one mountain, where we saw light at the border. We bypassed on the Western side headed towards the lights. When we approached, we branched where we walked through the bushes until we found ourselves in the Country. Out of the twenty people who got lost, only three of us made our way back and the rest got the worst of their lives there.

The mistake was that the person in front as we went on never made a signal to any person when he lost the sight of row. We got lost and suffered because of one person's mistake. People who are not flexible, always panic whenever encountered with challenges – they don't give a chance to learning, to plan when they are faced with circumstance. People who are not flexible are pushers – they apply force more than they apply knowledge hence they end up with no sense of directions to come out of situations. They always don't try to find out solutions to their problems, and the easiest solution they know very well is running away from problems. As they run away, they end up getting into the problem again and are easily worn out when encountered with difficulties. More so, they are not also easy people to deal with. They don't understand other people properly when there are difficulties. They are not transparent to their own being in any situation and this makes them be people who are easily defeated in any situation of changes. A flexible person changes his lifestyle and attitude with the likeliness of the contemporary situation for the reason of surviving in that situation.

A person like Nelson Mandela who today, the African Continent regards an icon, was successful in his political struggle in South Africa because he was a flexible person. When the Apartheid regime banned freedom of political parties – and the opposition politicians were being hunted by the apartheid regime, Nelson and his team (ANC) were flexible in their political activities. They did not force or resist the government. They shifted from gathering in open places during day times to secret places during the nights. That was how they survived and sustained ANC till they got what they struggled for- freedom of the people of South Africa.

Any changes we encounter comes with its force which is greater than us. It is like a hurricane - you cannot overpower it except if you survive in it. If you resist changes, you have taken a risk because the change will never spare you. During one of our annual conferences organized for the Sudanese Youth in Diaspora by JOSCHF in 2004, an organization I served in its' Executive Committee Board for about two years as General Secretary, an elder of the Sudanese Community in Kampala by name Samuel Udu, in his speech at the conference ended by saying, *"If you don't' Change, the change will change you."* With life, you need to be extremely careful, your target must be to survive in any situation and this will have to cause you to change in order to survive for the purpose of what you exist for, in this World. To be flexible is an act of being honest to your own self in a particular situation by changing your strategies, attitude, lifestyle etc; to fit properly in that particular period of time without being a victim or losing your purpose.

A person who is not flexible and not honest to their own self always digs their own grave by resisting change. Because change comes with a certain force that is overwhelming, they end up losing to change. In life, you have to be ready for any change, even some time in your profession. You won't insist that because you are an engineer, you will never work as a guard; or because your family is like this, therefore, you won't do that. To be flexible means to adapt to every situation. When our father died, it was a time for us to change in order to fit in that helpless situation and survive in it without losing focus and purpose. I was flexible; I did any kind of dirty work and never said to myself that I can't because my father was this or that. Whatsoever kind and nature of works I was doing, I never did it as a profession or trend of my life and never intended it to be so. I did it simply because I needed to survive. Flexibility has nothing to do with your profession, your family background or status. It has nothing to do with your academic qualifications, but, it has something to do with you as a person and the situation you are in. Flexibility is all about your wellbeing in that particular situation till when the storm is over and the situation becomes favourable to you.

In actual sense, flexibility is what many other scholars of life called *"shift Changes"*. The doctrine of this school of life is that life is not constantly the same, our lifestyles must shift to fit in any changes. This means that when there is a change in certainties, you need to shift yourself in accordance with that change. The world we live in, the policies, the technological inventions, politics, laws and trade changes from time to time as we face new challenges in this contemporary world. The ideal of flexibility or what the scholars of life called "shift Change" is that "Human changes with the World, they move with the World and they progress with the World – the same speed and the same directions". This made us (this generation) be successful in every aspect of life than the former generations. Therefore, where there is change, you have to shift to fit in that era in order to progress and be successful;

Forgive and forget; Forgiveness is a very important instrument of your own success. Your struggle with life and, future is in most cases hindered by your attitude of unwillingness to forgive those who wronged against you or put you in some difficult situation of life. If you don't forgive, you become bitter and your bitterness will always remind you of the past. This will make you become weary and weak in the thought of mind and attitude of the heart. This is the beginning of your failure. Lack of forgiveness reminds you constantly of your past situations. Therefore, you find yourself without time to think and plan for your future except grieving and feeling the pains of the situation you were put through by others.

Forgiveness is not only the right choice for success but also a principle of success. Forgiveness brings blessings, peace, happiness, and healing to you, which are strength to you to do and, accomplish that which is impossible for you. True freedom will only come from forgiveness. If you forgive, then your inner being feels free not only with others but also within yourself. Choosing to forgive does not necessarily mean that those wronged against you must first be sorry and repent of their mistakes and wrongs against you.

Sometimes forgiving is not necessarily going to that person and telling him or her, "I have forgiven you." It is just letting it go without putting him or her any more in your heart, and reaching again to him or her with love, kindness as well as relating with him or her as if he or she never wronged against you. Forgiveness can take place not only on a verbal basis but also on nonverbal basis through your conduct and the way you relate with or to those who wronged against you. With forgiveness, you are simply choosing to love in spite of the pain you are put through, to humble your pride and to let go of resentment and revenge and retribution.

Forgiveness is a principle of gratitude, giving, or meekness which is the key to success. If you don't have gratitude, humility, and generosity, success goes far away from you. The stage to forgive is a time when you are in your own courtroom, a presiding judge over the case that somebody wilfully or unintentionally hurts you – and you have to pass your judgments to forgive or not - the choice is yours and yours alone.

One thing you need to know is that the choice to forgive is for your own benefit and not for the benefit of your offender – forgiveness is a better choice because of its advantages for your success in life. Forgiveness makes you feel free and not to be bitter and misery because bitterness and misery are dangerous heart infections that may affect your whole being and kill your mentality. When your spirit is infected by lack of forgiveness – your life changes as misery and bitterness affect your creative thinking. With time, it will start to poison your spirit and mind, and by the end of the day, you just find yourself being defeated in life. Hence, you can no longer achieve what you are capable of doing or achieving in your lifetime.

In other words, you become mentally dead. People who are mentally dead are those that are capable of doing something great and better for themselves and the society, but because of circumstances in their life, they gave chance for their mind to be reduced to focus only on their miserable circumstance, and cannot think any more creatively. They no longer take chances of their common senses which are the power of creativity in humans and an engine for human success. Feelings are part of human life. The need for justice is part of the feeling in which forgiveness seems to be contradicting. This makes forgiveness to be one of the difficult choices and at the same time very hard for humans. Forgiveness goes against your sense of pride because it is lowering yourself to be humble and accommodative to all the wrongs done against you and to let it go as if nothing wrong happened to you. To let it go as if nothing hurts you, and even not suffering from this very consequence of the wrongs committed against you. To forgive someone means to put on the spirit of love, mercy, grace, kindness, truth and humility – despite the pains and hurts they put you through. This is the beautiful spirit of God. When you choose to forgive those who wronged against you, God becomes proud of you and blesses you with a new spirit of strength and courage to restart a new life of peace and happiness to inspire your success. With forgiveness, you are surrendering yourself, your pains and sufferings - including those who wronged against you to God; and acknowledging Him as the judge of mankind and His will for humans, because nothing that happens either good or bad without His will, and knowledge.

In my journey of struggle for a better life and future, I learnt how to forgive.

Of all the people, I forgave the man who might have possibly be responsible for the death of my father; I could remember one day we are traveling on foot - from Kaya to Otoka. When we reached Morobo, we went to his house just to say hello to him. Again after ten years when we met in 2003 during the Mundri Socio-economic Development Conference, I gave him a big hug before everyone and showed him respect not because of his military ranks but because of his age and it is my code to respect and be humble to others. I hugged him because I have not taken him in my heart. I had let whatsoever happened to go because. Only God knows everything and will judge the situation of the death of my father. In July 2016 when we were flashed out of Juba, from my base in Kudda, I coordinated his exit from Juba when he defected from the government to join armed opposition, the SPLA/ MM under the leadership of Dr. Riek Machar. He got me in Kudda while Dr. Riek Machar was in Kukutere in Dollo. I was the one who received him with a hug and though I was the only senior commander in the area, I left my own chair and gave it for him to sit on while I sat down on a mat to talk to him. I left my bathing water for him to bathe, and I made sure that the meal was served, and we ate from the same plate. I did that to prove to him that, I did not have any grudge against him. He was never comfortable, and I could see the fear in his face, but I looked at him and prayed deep inside my heart to God to continue giving me a heart to forgive any person that might have wronged against me as I forgave this man. I also prayed to God to make others forgive me where I had wronged them as I forgave others. After dinner, I arranged for him with those he came with to leave for a safe zone. I did not hate him, nor did I even have anything in my mind against him because I forgave him as God has commanded us to forgive others.

Forgiveness is very important for your own soul because it releases you from bitterness, and drags you gradually to forget your past and accommodate the present situations and to mind only the future life. If you don't forgive, you won't forget the situation and if you don't forget, you won't find peace inside you. I came across a young beautiful lady in South Africa whose heart was broken by her first boyfriend and would not let it go. This young lady at the age of fourteen broke her virginity to a man who fathered her first child, they had been in a relationship for five good years and then this man just dumped her and married another woman, she was left with a two-year-old son and it was a very difficult situation for her. She thought of committing suicide but it was not possible when she thought of her handsome son. Her lack of forgiveness to the father of her son made her be afraid of all men and her feelings toward men dragged her gradually to an extent that she became a lesbian. Lack of forgiveness dragged her from heterosexuality to homosexuality and this is where she seemed to have comfort and peace, though the hurts and the pains are still there.

Sacrifice; There is no success without sacrifice; to be successful, you first have to sacrifice something for something else and above all, you have to sacrifice your present for the future. Sacrifice is an act of waiving something valuable for the sake of something having more pressing claim; sacrifice in a broad sense is an act of using your own valuables for something of more worth.

Something interesting about Islamic Religion is the idea of Jihad which is a practical life of every Muslim. Many people - especially non-Muslims have the wrong perceptions of Jihad which in most cases, they associate jihad with terrorism and war. The idea of jihad in Islam is quite different and every genuine Muslim intends to live his or her life as Mujihid for the cause of Allah and his or her beliefs. Supposedly Muslim can become a Mujihid by what he has, including his abilities. The ideal of Jihad in Islam is classified into five; - Jihad bi Nefis (Self), Jihad bi Ilm (knowledge), Jihad bi Mali (wealth) and Jihad bi Wakid (Time). Jihad is an idea of sacrifice of any Muslims for the cause of his faith to the God he believes in and worships. Jihad is the most practical thing in Islam. This makes Muslims be successful in every aspect of their religion and their individual life. This makes me love the teachings of Islam. To be successful in life, you need to sacrifice something for something else worth more.

In fact, throughout history, every hero, every great person and every successful person either in public or private, sacrificed something that paid him to be a hero, a great person or a successful person. This sacrifice perhaps, includes his very self, time, Knowledge and Wealth for the cause of something great, which in turn made him be successful, great and a hero. The idea of sacrifice is not to sacrifice your own future for the present or something worth for something of less worth. It is not also to sacrifice your own life for others - the idea is to sacrifice what is of less worth in life for what is of more worth in life; to save your own life (at a time when you really feel no longer like living on this earth rather than to die), for the sake of others.

The idea of sacrifice is not to die for others, but to sacrifice to live for the sake of others. You don't die to save others, but you live to save others because saving others is continuity of the purpose of existence but not of death. In fact, throughout my life as an orphan – there are lots of sacrifices I have made and all was for the future and the cause of success. From my childhood life to my teenage life – there was nothing that I ever enjoyed like my fellow children and teenagers. The time when other children after schools were playing games, I was busy working in a workshop repairing bicycles or other people's shoes, selling Roasted Nuts, or firewood. The time when other teenagers are going to clubs, drinking liquors, smoking and moving here and there with girls, I was busy with books or working. I had no life – for I sacrificed everything for the course of my future and success. There are times in life, I became overwhelmed. Life became useless and all that I could see, think and feel was death; I am at a crossroad to commit suicide; but what could I gain after all if I committed suicide? Nothing! So, I had to sacrifice to live because I knew when I live, my life will be worth more to others than when I die.

One of my greatest sacrifices ever in my adulthood was when I sacrificed myself and love. When I got into South Africa where I had to start life all again alone and from nothing, I got a Job but the demand was high- I had to plan for my own future and at the same time got some political tasks to accomplish. There were real-life pressures on me from every aspect of life. I was working day and night. I had no time to rest and go out for fun as a normal person. I knew that I would not make it alone. I needed somebody to talk to, to smile at and above all, somebody to hold my hands and say, "I Love you."

My life was so miserable. I came across many beautiful ladies but I decided to block my heart from Love and abstained because I never wanted to be distracted. I knew that Love is a responsibility, it is workable and to get involved in any love relationship would cost my success again. I had no business with girls. I was as I was when I was still a teen. Because of my lifestyle of having nothing to do with ladies, my best Swazi girlfriend called me a 'Coward'. I definitely agreed that I was a 'Coward', but not for nothing. I was coward to girls because getting into any relationship means accepting responsibilities that I was not ready for.

More painful was when I sacrificed my true love and a woman who I initially dreamt of spending the rest of my life with. In my struggle for success, I had to sacrifices her simply because I knew that was the only thing I had to do if I would ever achieve my goal. She was not only a true woman that I loved and wanted to spend the rest of my life with – till death; but also the only person that I depended on, for any help. I sacrificed her love because I needed peace of mind if I had to be successful. A man will never be successful or achieve all that he dreams of attaining while under family stress, and having a sense of culpability of seeing that person whom you loved, suffering emotionally as if, all your efforts to make her happy, loving and making her proud is not being recognized. Of course, women have that special emotional need where they need to feel loved and cared for. They also have that worry when a man is not close to them because they feel insecure as if some other women out there will snatch her lover. Because she was not able to understand my situation, I had to tell her, 'Darling, I am sorry, but you can move on with life, if that can give you happiness." It was a painful decision because I knew from that single decision, now, I would lose someone that I loved so much and never wished to live without in my life – but then, I had to, if at all I wanted to be successful. I needed that peace of mind and a life free from stress if I wanted to remain focused on my struggle for a better life and future.

Life is not all about being with a woman all the time in a room to look at each other and having sex. It is about securing a sustainable future free from threats and wants. I had to enter into a forest to burn charcoal for business which was a very difficult task. All the same, I had to, if I wanted to get funds for restarting my life and implementing my projects. It was in the forest where I started talking to myself about life. It was that conversations between the real me, and the outer spirits within me – that intended to corrupt me. It was in that forest and that difficult moment that my attitudes toward humans and life started to change. But, it was also in that forest that I said to myself for the very first time in life, "I am a Man." That single confession that I am a man-made me to be a real man who can endure any difficult situation and envision that good future is only for real men. In life, you will never be successful if you fear to sacrifice yourself, to sacrifice something you like in life for something you valued in life. It is only in sacrifice that man becomes successful. To sacrifice something never means to miss something in life. There are some things that one will never miss as long as you are still alive on this earth. You will never miss smoking and drinking, Love and sex and definitely going to clubs, the lists goes on and on.

If you sacrifice love or sex or drinks or smoking today for the sake of what is more important, which will give you a real-life and happiness, tomorrow, you will still get all that you sacrificed yesterday, and perhaps a little better than, what you sacrificed.

Intelligence; All mankind has the same dream- that is to be successful in life. However, it is only the intelligent that lives their dream of success true in life. According to the English Webster's New World Dictionary definition,

> An intelligent person is a person who uses the faculty of reason in solving problems, directing conduct; any degree of keenness of mind, cleverness, shrewdness, etc; a person with the ability to acquire and retain knowledge; mental ability, a person with the ability to respond quickly and successfully to a new situation; a person who uses the faculty of reason in solving problems, perception, discernment: a person with the ability to reason or understand or to perceive relationships, differences, etc.; a person with the power of thought; mind.

An intelligent person lives the present life for the future life; the present life is meaningless to him and all that he cares much about is the unseen future life. The unseen future is the first priority and the focus of the intelligent person, but not the past or the present life. An intelligent person always takes advantage of the present life with all its challenges to acquire happiness and to allow the present life with all its implications to take him throughout his lifetime and thereafter to the last destination to his creator with happiness. To be intelligent means to live your present life for the future through planning for a better future, and never being reckless with the present life, which is the core beginning of the future.

An intelligent person attempts all his living for one single purpose - his happiness, joy and peace by the end but not at the present. The end is of greater concern to an intelligent than the present life. Thus an intelligent person lives for the two unfolded future of mankind:

First the future life on this World; a man should not live his life all for the present life because you can determine the present by feeling or seeing it, unlike the future. The future is totally invisible and you don't know how good or bad it will be for you. You can't determine what will unfold in the future; hence you have to be careful about it, than with the present. An intelligent person will never be deceived by the present life pleasures; he will never spend his earnings for the present pleasures of life, but carefully investing his present earnings for the future. Intelligent people don't work hard for the present pleasures of life but for future pleasures. Their lifetime goal is to leave a legacy in the life of others, their family, society and the World they live in that is, legacy of peace, joy and happiness. Your life must be guided by the future you visualize. Every aspect of your living in the present time must reflect your dreams for the future. This will guide you not to be crazy with present life even benefit you in future life. Living for the future simply means to prioritize your lifestyle – doing first what is very vital for your future and then what is vital for the present in second place. The mistake many young people make is that, when they reach a certain age, they become mad with life and change their lifestyle immediately as if life, is coming to an end. Therefore, you either enjoy it now or miss it in your lifetime because there is no life in the future! Yes, you can enjoy it right now but what about the future? Will you enjoy this life present life and bear a future life of suffering? An intelligent person always asks himself of the future but this is not the matter with many people nowadays. Many people intend to live their lives for the present and as a result, our contemporary society is crippled. Poverty is increasing too fast and social crime is becoming the order of the day; hence we compete with life but we do not catch it. We not only lose and fail but find ourselves in the same situation of life. Indeed, Life is useless and meaningless because if you enjoy it to the maximum today, and tomorrow you suffer, then the life you enjoyed yesterday was useless and meaningless. If you were a happy man yesterday and today you are unhappy man, you won't call yourself a happy person because that happiness has passed away with life yesterday while today is another life with its challenges and suffering facing you. Therefore, your past enjoyment and happiness become history, the present turns into reality, full of regrets and the future is filled with worries and troubles. This is all because you are not intelligent in living your life in the best way through investing it for your lifetime on this World. Therefore, to have a better and happy end of life is the struggle and purpose of living of an intelligent person. – He works hard to earn a living not only for the present but for the future life. Thus, intelligent people invest their present life for the future and the end of their lives is happiness and Peace. They ensure that those around them are in total peace and happiness. Thereafter, they call themselves successful because there is nothing they worry about now about tomorrow. Therefore, your earnings and present life should be an investment for your own future, including the future of your family and community. The ideal of investment of present earnings for future peace and happiness is a principle of intelligent people; hence they end up living their life for community services through lending their hands, skills and resources for the benefit of their community because the happiness and peace of others means theirs too.

Secondly, the future life after this World; an intelligent person is one with a sense of his existence of where he came from and the final destination of his life when his contract of life in this World will have expired and after breathing his final breath in death. Above all, he is a person with a sense of the existence of a supernatural being greater than him, who is above all natural beings, in whose lies the life and destiny of all mankind, and that is Allah (Ta'ala). An intelligent person is one with knowledge of life after death and is more concerned about his life after death than the present temporary earthly life. The World that you live in, with all its pleasures is temporary. It ends when you die, but physical death does not mean the end of life because there is a life after death and that is the greatest life that you must long for. It is eternal life and in that new World, everything therein, is everlasting and this is where God stays. To be part of the new World with God means that you have to be absolutely good and do good things only with your life when still alive in this World because that is a place for good people with God. The place for bad people is hell with Satan. Hence an intelligent person's desire is only to be in good places with good people and only to see good things.

This guides every intelligent human to not only to do good things for themselves but to others and the world they live in. Success is not measured by how much you possessed in your lifespan, but the positive impact of your life. Intelligence is a core foundation, hence when a person lacks intelligence, by the end of his life, he will not be considered successful in life.

My struggle for success was not only for the worldly life but also for the life that is to come after death, it was my spiritual struggle for everlasting life with God when I die. My dogma is to be successful not only for this World but for the World to come. I worked hard to earn my living and survive in this world, not for this world, but for God. I spent hours and hours reading God's Word and making Dua *(prayers)* to God and it is in God's word where I found my wisdom for living. God's word guided my life and I never wronged any person – even when sometimes I found myself in a company of wrong people, and mafias. I lived differently from them in their midst – to an extent that most of them regarded me to be boring and living like a dead person without life simply because I don't drink, smoke and was not on drugs, not womanizing and fighting like them. I was proud to be called all these sorts of names because I am original to myself and I never forged who I am not. My concern for the future life and particularly life after death was my guiding principles and it kept me safe, thus my foundation for success.

Throughout history, I heard and read about great people, who worked hard in all sorts of life and came to the top and became national figures. Some as heads of state and examples could be like the late President Saddam Hussein of Iraq, the late Mabuto Sessa Seko of the Democratic Republic of Congo, the late Id Amin of Uganda, and Late Muhammed Gadafi of Libya, including the former President Omer El Bashir of Sudan. Those people were successful because in the first place, they attained a top position where many tried but, couldn't reach. However, because they lacked intelligence, the end of their life, was just a big failure. Their end was no longer as successful as for politicians or leaders or persons in their own communities. Their end was a failure. Without intelligence, you might work hard and get whatsoever you want in life, be a millionaire and on top of the World, but the end of your life will be unhappiness and suffering.

POLITICS, LOVE AND COURAGE IN THE FACE OF DURESS

Life is costly by nature, it costs to destroy, as well as to save – but the profit is where life and relationship are saved.

Foundation of my political will

Coercion in society is the cause of fear, which makes life vulnerable, but only courage and love can conquer duress and fear in our lives, and save us, as well our individual human relationship with others in this World. Therefore, when encountered with threats and fear, outfit on courage and love because these are the only shield we can use to survive in any situation. We are all human created by one creator with equal life but our lifestyle different from each other because of some situations. Hence, every lifestyle that we live, has its foundation and every choice we make in life is driven by a situation that becomes our experiences and force behind our lifestyle. The foundation of my political choice was from a small town of Kaya in South Sudan, where I got not only changed, but also promised myself to have nothing to do with the regime of SPLA/ MSPLA/M. I became committed in our contemporary South Sudanese politics, not because I was born that way, but because circumstances caused me. My deep political hatred to SPLA/ MSPLA/ M and the cause of my political ambitions came as a result of the following reasons. First, my physical humiliation by the abuse of power by the SPLA/ M Commander, Magar Akech; second, an attempt to massacre us, the entire family at home by the SPLA/ M fighter; thirdly, the circumstance surrounding the death of my father; fourthly, my physical torture by the bodyguards of Commander James Wani Igga inside his Compound and fifthly, my survival after an attempted murder by SPLA/M major. These occurrences influenced and made me have a strong will to fight for the establishment of a nation where all humans are free from any threats and wants. Though by then we were in the SPLA/ M Liberated areas and called ourselves SPLA/ M, I was not one, in my inner being, I was a rebel against SPLA/ M, only that, I had no opportunity to defect, and fight SPLA/ MSPLA/ M. I had always supported Sudanese Government in my heart, and during the time of leadership crisis in the SPLA/ MSPLA/ M between Riek Machar and John Garang, I had secretly supported any movement that was by then against SPLA/ MSPLA/ M and the leadership of John Garang. Unfortunately, by then - at that age, I was never exposed to real politics until 2001 when I came to Kampala and joined the high institution of learning. It was in Kampala when I became in touch with some Sudanese politicians. Of course, if there was anyone that exposed me to the real political industry as well as to intelligence services, it was never a Sudanese but a Pakistan National, Sheikh Khan Taqvi. A man who influenced me to understand that, the solution to every contemporary situation, is in the very hands of mankind. I remember one day when we were in a very deep discussion with him. He explained to me how evil some people are – desperately struggling to rule this world, and said, "The problem of your Country (Sudan) is the making of the Americans and the Europeans.

They are just using John Garang not for the benefit of the people of South, but for their selfish benefits, and after they get what they want, they will deal with him." he continued on lecturing me, and what actually pushed me harder was when he asked me whether I know that, I am suffering not because there is a war in South Sudan, but because of the SPLA/ M and John Garang. He became so clear and pointed me saying, "My boy, it is you who is suffering while your leaders are not! They have money, they eat and sleep well, their children having the best education while you are suffering and struggling to get tuition fee, you are struggling for what to eat and even where to sleep." He paused for some moments and said in a very soft voice, "*Do not worry, my boy because every situation has its' solution, but it will all depend on the choice we make as individuals because the solution to every problem is always with man, and not God as many people think.*"

Henceforth, I never had peace. I started developing some great ambitions and that was the beginning of a new start in my life. This brought me to a new life where I became involved in some secret service business for a while. But I was more interested in politics than in Private Secret Services, even though I developed an interest to amplify my contacts and establish meaningful intelligence Contacts, including direct contact with the Sudanese Security apparatus in Khartoum. My motive was not actually Security Services but to use any contacts in that arena for political benefit– for building myself. I was the same outside me, but inside, I had changed. I spent my day time with those of Eng. Jackson Khamis and late Juma Mamuru but they never knew who I was and what I did.

We could converse, but they never knew that, I had signed up to the Secret Service organization in the world of mafias, and even if it would make me evil, by then, I was ready and willing, as long as this would help me achieve what I intended to achieve.

Unfortunately Sheikh Khan Taqv, due to the security situation, he had to depart before September 11, 2001, from Uganda to an unknown location, and without him, my dreams vanished as those in his cycle that he had left behind, instead of building me up, plotted to kill me on the Night of 9th September 2001 not because I was evil but to end up the deal between me and them. I then moved and started to share accommodation with Barnabas Balabala. More so, my new chief was not interested in developing me; but using me. Therefore, due to the high pressures from every angle of my life, I quit studies for a while because I could not handle it all at once by then.

I remained in Kampala until 2005 when I returned to Sudan. By then I had got a contract with IAS in Jonglei. This never worked out well. I returned to Kampala and re-established my political contacts but it never worked well too, so I had to go to Malawi for security reasons. In Malawi, I continued with my political work and this time I became connected directly with an armed rebel movement in South Sudan that was anti-SPLA/ MSPLA/ M and the leadership of Salva Kiir. Besides this, I also got connected with a Somali Businessman, politician and Mafia, Sheikh Ahmed, and my connection with him was strictly geared by business prospective for mutual benefits.

Terrorism accusation and Insecurity

I was in Malawi until 2008 when I developed some cycle of political coercion and insecurity threats, which caused my kidnapping in July that year. My insecurity was caused by my activities for Sheikh Ahmed. His opponents targeted me because of my professionalism. I became unsafe in Malawi. I had to leave Malawi for South Africa, in search of Peace and Security, which I had lost in Malawi. I was welcomed by my cousin Isaac who had been in South Africa for some time. There, I met comrade Mike who was an active Community member and had taken up a project of organizing our South Sudanese community in South Africa to be productive, both, in terms of the welfare of our members in South Africa, as well to create coexistence for the national course. His effort brought about the formation of the Sudanese Community of Southern Africa "SUCOSA." He was elected the Secretary-General and I became his deputy.

Though I was serving in the Community office, I continued with my political activism, which brought the conflict of interest and I was released from the community office within a few months of service, as the organization by nature is pro SPLA/ M, which I was opposed to. Furthermore, my relationship with the SPLA/ M Chapter as well the Government of South Sudan Liaison office in South Africa was sour, as I intended to use the community office, for political purpose against SPLA/ M and Government of South Sudan, while Liaison office was by then not only financier to the community activities in South Africa, but also manipulating the community to be pro-SPLA/ M only.

By then, politically, for sure, we do have disagreements but socially, we are one in every course as a community. Even with my cousin (Isaac) whom we shared the same accommodation; who was a member of SPLA/M but also by then got involved in Human Intelligence Business with other foreign missions in South Africa.

However, after some time, my Cousin and the SPLA/M Chapter Chairman, Mr. Samuel became so close; but I never expected that any of them would pose a security threat to me, even if it happened that, we were of different political ideals and movements. I trusted both of them and I thought that their close relationship had to do with the security business as Mr. Samuel also ran the private security industry in Rustenburg Municipality. However, I got a bit suspicious due to a string of daily cell phone conversation between the two even at night hours, and some series of private meetings between the two. At first, I thought the two comrades could be in serious business deals though, I could not figure out the nature of their trade. I am not that kind of a person who likes to put his nose in other people's private affairs. So, I never intended to interfere with their business but I became eager to know what was happening. To know the nature of their private business was very important to me because you cannot stay with a person at the same house while you don't know that person's other side of life. To know the private business of the person you stay with is not actually an interference in their private life, but being security cautions, just in case of uncertainties, if you are wise enough because it is for your own safety reasons.

So one night, after he received a cell phone call from Samuel, he went out and they talked for about 10 minutes.

I started wondering. When he came in, I asked him about the nature of his business with Samuel. I was cautious to know since Samuel is the Head of the SPLA/M Chapter; someone so close to the Liaison office may be something of interest to me, in terms of political know-how of plans and activity of SPLA/M or Liaison office, and other classified information. He paused for a moment and then told me that, he and Samuel had some business with National Intelligence Services (NIS), the State Security Apparatus of South Africa Government. "What business?" I asked. He said that there were some Pakistanis in New Town, Johannesburg who were terrorists. I then cautioned him as a brother to be extremely careful especially when his human intelligence business involves counterterrorism activities. I had some basic knowledge of human intelligence services, so I gave some fundamental advice on intelligence services, not knowing that I was one of the terror suspects in their list. I never knew that they were working against me. However, I became extremely alert because, on a number of occasions, there was an attempt by an unknown user to infiltrate my laptop. I never suspected that it was an attempt by him to search for any useful data and use it against me as substantiation. Of course, I did not have any sensitive data that could get me into trouble. I only had lecture notes because, by then I was an assistant lecturer in one of the private Colleges in Johannesburg, where Joseph Alia was the Principal. Therefore, I had no classified data on my laptop, apart from some photos. However, since I was always cautious of uncertainties, I had security settings because I never wanted some stranger to use my laptop and infiltrate my data without my knowledge. Conversely, one day when I was going through my photo album in the Computer; I noticed that two photographs in which I had posed with a certain person were missing.

I knew somebody infiltrated by laptop and might have deleted the photos, or instead of copying it, he or she had saved it in another device. I tried to find out who might have used my laptop, but I got no answer. So I let it go. I only changed the security settings. I never suspected that the two buddies were working against me, and had accused me as a terrorist agent, to the National Intelligence Service (NIS) of South Africa. They did so not because I was actually one, but because of their individual selfish ambitions for power positions and Wealth.

As a person with an intelligence background, I was very fast to uncover all their dirty plots, not only against me but also against some individuals that I happened to know, like Mr. Joseph Ali, an educationist and Principal of the college where I used to lecture. They accused Joseph Ali of smuggling terrorist operatives in South Africa, through educational purpose that he was offering admission letters to those terrorists and processing Student's visa and permits for them to come and stay in South Africa, as Students. My life was under threat – with fear of the possibility of arrest and deportation by the South African Government, and at the same time, fear of the regime of SPLA/ M in South Sudan, based upon my political activities against SPLA/ M Regime. As a matter of fact, there was nothing I wrong did to any of them, but they just turned against me and accused me of what I didn't know or activities I was never involved in. But, this is the reality of this world where any person can betray even if you don't have any misunderstanding with that person. Because of this, you don't have to trust humankind since the human heart is too deceitful to be trusted.

To trust humankind is to take a risk and therefore, all that you need is to love humankind for what, and who they are and hope that, they are, and will remain good enough to you, and never hurt you at a given moment. I never believed that those two would raise false accusations against me. This shows that humankind is too complicated to understand their hearts and mind even if you eat together, hence your enemy is not that person who is far away from you but the one near to you. Your enemy is the one you are eating and staying together with because this is the very person who will betray and kill you at any time. With such accusation they raised against me, politically, I did agree because I was against SPLA/ M regime, hence the accusation was politically motivated so as to put me in trouble with South African Authorities just like I was in trouble with authorities in Malawi before. But was this evil intention of accusing me of terrorism politically motivated! What about Isaac? He was the guy who never showed any interest in politics, in all his activities since we had been staying together. So, what was his interest to put my life in danger? I then realized that, the accusation was not politically motivated but it had to do with their individual selfish ambitions which were all about money for Isaac, while for Samuel, it was all about power and position within South Africa Security apparatus and his political career in South Sudan as a security expert. They never accused me because I did something wrong against them but because of their individual selfish ambitions. They were willing to destroy me, or any other person, in order to reach their aspiration in life.

It is never bad to have ambitions in life, but it is dangerous to have ambition without means to materialize it, because it will become the cause of evil deeds and plots.

People don't turn against you and come up with evil intentions against you because you are wrong, or they hate you. They may sometimes not hate you but can hurt you if it means that hurting you can help them achieve their ambitions. Therefore, your greatest fear should not be the person but ambition in the person – because any ambition with no realistic means to achieve its' status, it can turn the person to be evil, to destroy you at any time as long they think destroying you can materialize their dreams. Hence, unrealistic ambition in individuals or groups is a problem as in most cases becomes the causes of our human insecurity and threats. It was the unrealistic ambition of man to be like God, to have knowledge of what is right and what is wrong; that caused the fall of man in the Garden of Eden. Ambition is what caused Judas to betray Jesus as it was clear that, there was never any misunderstanding between Jesus and Judas or any of the Disciples. Because Judah has ambitious for money, he never knew what he was doing when he sold Jesus out for some thirty denarii. All he thought was money and didn't mind whether his actions would hurt Jesus and the entire Ministry. Unfortunately, when Jesus was arrested and sentenced to death, Judas became remorseful and even returned the money, but it was too late. So, he hanged himself. Hence, ambition for money or something is what causes robbery or even killing of people in our society, because since one has the desire for something, he doesn't care whether he hurts any person.

I am not against having ambition because it is natural and never sin or a crime; ambition is a great thing because it is a power behind every success.

However, you need to be cautious so that, your ambition does not turn to be malevolent, to cause harm to others, or make you evil among others in society. In fact, people don't become evil because they are born evil by nature, but because they have conceived some unrealistic ambitions, in the process of their life, thus, they have to give birth to some evil actions that affect others today. Unrealistic ambition is the nature of Lucifer, and that is why the unrealistic ambition becomes the cause of evils happening in our contemporary society. Lucifer was an archangel of God in Heaven who conceived the unrealistic ambition to be greater than God. This unrealistic ambition led Lucifer to sin and be thrown out by God. Therefore, the world is suffering from the result of the unrealistic ambition of Lucifer. Hence; you can never rule out the possibility of evil in any person as long as humans have ambitions since you can also not rule out the possibility of people on this earth from having ambitions.

However, in a situation where others may turn against you without a just course, never also try to find out reasons why they turned against you; because the more you try to reason, the more you will find yourself innocent and become irate to be against them too, which will make you and them be evil at same time. Never forget that we are living in the sinful world and therefore, any person can turn against you at any time. But when others turn against you, let love and courage rule you because this is the only way – to present yourself, and face the reality without revenge, and to bring those against you to understand the truth, and come back to you when that time comes.

Love is all about being passionate to somebody even when that person has wronged against you while courage is the ability to face reality within the atmosphere of fear without being taken by the temptation to be arrogant that will leads to retaliation. Though this serious accusation labeled against me created an unsafe living environment for me in South Africa, I was confident of winning because I was innocent. There was no sufficient evidence presented to NIS to substantiate terrorist changes against me to warrant my arrest and detention. In spite of these accusations, I was sure of winning the two because I had a very clear strategy that was never to be against any of my accusers, but to face every single stage with "pure love," and "utmost courage." This was because I believe that, love and courage is the only medicine I can use, to bring my accusers and the world not only to believe me but also to convict them of their evil as they will see the innocence in me. Therefore, during that time, I never turned against any of them; I loved them and was courageous to meet them, stay with them in the same home, and ate with them on the same table. My sincere love and paramount courage turned them to acknowledge their own individual mistakes, and above all, to confess to me what was at first as their top-secret, though their confessions came in form of counteraccusations, and counter blames of each other.

My love continues to bridge the gap and draw us nearer to each other as courage endures new hope of oneness. At a time when the South Africa Police Services from Tactical Unit, as well as detective, came to look for me, I was informed that, after my return from my short trip to Empangeni in Kwazulu Natal, I was so optical that, it is the so-called terrorism case and therefore, this troubled me, not because I have guilty but because I knew Mr. Samuel was well connected politically, as well as financially stable. Therefore, since he had already been evil to me and accused me of terrorism, I assumed that he could use his political connections and financial resources to ensure his goal comes true in the future. That was my fear and worry because on the other hand, I was very poor and my contact was very poor by then, which meant, justice would not be on my side.

So, when I returned home from my trip and my Zimbabwean friend informed me of the incident of police officers who came to look for me, I told him, "*I am an innocent person. Besides, I am a law-abiding person and therefore, I did nothing wrong in South Africa or anywhere in the World*", I was saying this with a pure conscience. I paused for some seconds and told him, "*If there is any problem that caused the Police to be looking for me, I believe it could be the so-called terrorism case.*" I narrated to him how I was accused as a terrorist and assured him that; this could be the case -nothing else, because I trust in myself.

However, after I finished the conversation with him, my heart became broken. I experienced a great fear, but my courage overpowered the fear so as to face the reality – while trusting in God alone to see me through that situation.

I took a deep breath and had internal prayers for courage and strength, and then I phoned Samuel his cell phone was on voicemail; I tried Comrade Atlas King who by then came from Cape Town and was staying with Samuel, Mr. Atlas King told me that, Samuel had gone to Zambia. I knew Comrade Atlas knew everything and therefore I told him about the incident that Police were looking for me, with the expectation that, he would at least tell me what he knew about that matter.

Unfortunately, Comrade Atlas denied having the knowledge of the situation. More so, He told me, he was not in Rustenburg when I asked to meet with him. However, the following day in the morning, he phoned me and told me that, he was in Rustenburg but never gave me any details of the matter, he rather asked to know my plans; I told him, that I intended to go to the Police Station to find out what the matter was. He then volunteered and asked me to wait for him so that he could accompany me but I dodged him because I intended to face the matter alone, to avoid exposition of my plans – since he had already shown some signal of working together with Samuel on that project to have me arrested. My conviction was that because comrade Atlas stayed with Samuel at home or had a close alliance with. The reason for this was that comrade Atlas had already taken the battle of Samuel on himself as far as having Comrade Mike arrested in Pretoria, and also plotted for the arrest of Isaac too. Comrade Mike was simply a political victim of his own political ambition who wanted to unseat Samuel from the chairmanship of the SPLA/ M Chapter, that period.

So when I phoned him, it was not because I needed him, but because I wanted to find out from him not only the whereabouts of Samuel since his cell phone was off but also to obtain some valuable information in regard to the reason the police was looking for me because I knew, he and Samuel were best friends who were both Chapter Executive Committee of SPLA/M in South Africa.

So, I went to the Rustenburg Police Station alone to find out what the matter was. To my surprise, there was no case against me, which means that those officers were not from Rustenburg Police Station. I then phoned this Zimbabwean friend who then gave me the contact of the Detective officer, who was in charge of the operation by then, I phoned this detective who happened to be from Tlhabane Police Station and suggested for me to meet him at BP Garage in Town but I objected, referring to meet him at Rustenburg Police Station for Security reason, based on the nature of the situation. I was afraid, maybe, those could be fake Police who would kidnap and hurt me. He was also an understandable officer, who agreed upon my proposition Therefore, we were able to meet the following day at Rustenburg Police Station. To my incredulity, it was no longer a case of terrorism as I expected. I was accused by Samuel that, *I was a terror suspect, and that I was conspiring with some Pakistanis to kill him because of his services for NIS, on counter-terrorist investigation.* I gave my statement and since there was no evidence to link me with any of these connives, I was declared innocent and walked out from the Police Station not only free, but also happy because I knew, that this meant the dead-end to the issue of terrorism, as well as a great Victory over Samuel, and the current insecurity threats I was encountering in the Country from NIS.

After the return of Samuel from Lusaka - Zambia, I called him because he had some dues which he never cleared when I was doing some work for him in his security industry. By then his relationship with Isaac was rotten and they had started to fight, and counter accuse each other. Isaac felt that Samuel not only betrayed him but used him for his (Samuel's) benefit because he never got any token from NIS as they agreed. As I stated, Isaac was after money and Samuel after power position within the security industry. It became a big problem between the former comrades. Samuel then lied to me saying that Isaac had made him believe in the nonsense of terrorism. He then told me about my photographs which he said were in the possession of NIS. More so, he said that if I wanted to leave South Africa, I should let him know so that he could help me leave because it would be difficult for me to leave without being cleared by NIS. Isaac had also told me all I needed to know about this matter of terrorism.

Those are the comrades who teamed up against me. I wondered why, now that they were confessing, and involving in counteraccusation of each other to me. It is simply because I never developed antagonism against them, but I remained friendly to them. In any situation where people turned against you without justifiable reasons, let your love shine to them. Never hate or seek vengeance, because hatred and vengeance will never solve any problems but will make it worse. We live in a world that is conquered with evils, where any person can conceive evil plots against you without a just course. However, the only medicine is to continue loving and having the courage to live with such people, if at all you have to save your human society or relationship. Therefore, Love and Courage are the remedies that heal human relationships, as well as any human misunderstanding which might have been brought by conflict of interests as a result of some unrealistic ambitions. It is only with love and courage that we can afford to keep human society together as one. Your love and courage to face those who are against you and to be at peace and unity with them is the bridge that links you together. This makes love and courage the core foundation of reconciliation for humankind. As a matter of fact, today, in spite of all these false accusations, I am happy that between Samuel and I and between Isaac and I there is nothing such as hatred but mutual understanding and reasoning as well as a good spirit for each other, even when we disagree.

I hope that, even as they will read this, they will develop the spirit of reasoning and not take it personally, because the truth must be known for the goodness of our society – especially to those who find themselves in such a situation.

Human beings are ambitious, which may sometimes cause problems amongst them. But when we act with mutual love and mutual courage for one another, especially those against us, we will withstand the greatest of any challenge and political disagreement.

The kismet of my asylum status and deportation threats

Indeed, in South Africa, apart from the threats of the terrorism accusation; politically, I was never safe from the Government of SPLA/ M because, if they would get an opportunity to annihilate me, they would do it since the political field is never an arena where you can have clemency on your enemy. Therefore, I never wanted to take any chance; especially at the time when South African's Department of Home Affairs refused to renew my political asylum permit for an unjustified reason that, "they could not find my file in their Data Base". I had been in South Africa for five years and extended my permit several times. So, how come that, they could not find my file in their database?

It never made any logic. So, I became worried about this decision. On my side at that time, the option was only to leave South Africa, for the fear of the possibility of arrest and deportation by the South African Authority, which was what South Sudan Embassy in South Africa was looking for since they wanted to have me killed, or arrested and deported to South Sudan.

My worry was partially caused by the accusation labeled against me as a terrorist because I thought, maybe, the motive for such a decision of declining to renew my asylum might have been prompt by the accusation. But then, I realized that this might not be the case of terrorism but my political activities because of the prior incidence by Home Affairs to rebuff renewing my permit. I recall when Samuel returned from South Sudan. By then, our relationship had normalized and there was an exchange of political and intellectual ideas between him and I. He cautioned me to be extremely careful even from any of our Equatorian Community members in South Africa because he was in the Embassy. Those people were plotting to have me deported or eliminated due to my political activities and contacts herein South Africa. According to him, he mentioned precisely my mail to the Croatia Ambassador in Pretoria. I then believed him because I had for sure written to the Croatia Ambassador. But the question was, how South Sudan Embassy came across the mail. I guess the Croatia embassy official might have had leaked the letter because there was no other way it could be disclosed since I did things alone by myself, without any external hand.

Therefore, with the incident where Home Affairs refused to renew my Asylum Permit, I became suspicions and I believed that if I remained in South Africa without any valuable documents, this would give an opportunity for those with evil plots against me to have me arrested and possibly deported. This was very dangerous for my safety as a rebel and a person who was involved in a series of political activities against the regime in Juba.

I then departed South Africa for the Republic of Seychelles with the intention of applying for political asylum, since it wouldn't be safe for me to return to South Sudan. Unfortunately, the Government of the Republic of Seychelles not only denied me political asylum but also deported me to South Africa, even though I produced to them the necessary documents to prove that it was unsafe for me to return to South Africa since the South Africa Government refused to extend my asylum permit to stay there. I tried to negotiate with the Seychelles Authority to allow me voluntarily leave the Country. But they refused and I was kept in custody at the Central Police State in Victoria for five days and then deported to South Africa in an escort of two Security Agents from Seychelles International Security Agency.

Upon arrival at OR Tembo Airport in Johannesburg, I was handed to South Africa Immigration and was issued with a warrant of deportation to South Sudan, and then taken to Kempton Park Police Station for two weeks – where I tried to establish contacts with UNHCR and other legal institution. All the same, all was in vain and could not secure any help. I was then transferred to Lindela Holding Facility which serves as a deportation centre. In Lindela, I fund a thousand plus other foreign nationals in the facility, who waited for deportation.

It is from Lindela, I believed that being in a foreign country, no matter how right you might be, you could still be considered wrong. There, the authorities could real torture and abuse foreigners at the centre, and you could not complain because there was not established mechanisms in place to report any abuse by the officials. I stayed at the centre for about three months where communication was not allowed and I could not inform or try to follow up the possibility of either being released or allowed to voluntarily leave the Country. Things were really tough for me. I never knew how I could be released due to the lack of access to communication with any other officials from the centre. Besides, my case seemed to be complicated and the human rights institution that used to help people at the centre seemed to have a challenge in helping me, though I can't understand what the problem was. I was really traumatized. To worsen the matter, one early morning, the guard came and told me to be prepared because I would be taken to the Embassy to sign an Emergency Travel Document for my deportation to South Sudan. I actually had no time for any preparation. I just followed him to the office where two immigration officers took me to the Embassy to sign the Emergency Travel Document. The funny thing was that instead of being taken directly to the Republic of the South Sudan Embassy (though they know very well that I am South Sudanese) they decided to take me first to the Embassy of the Republic of Sudan. At the Embassy of the Republic of Sudan, I refused to come out since that was a foreign embassy, but I was forced to come down and we all walked into the office and met with the Consulate.

After some inquiry, the Sudanese Consulate told other Immigration officers who were with me in the office, "This man is one of us, but politically, we are no longer one as they have their own Country (South Sudan)." To my amazement, he affirmed, but asked, "Then why do you bring him here?" The consulate became concerned with my situation and told the South African immigration, "This guy has insecurity problem back at home because he is a member of the opposition. Deporting him may put his life at risk from his government." The immigration officer never wanted to pay attention to vital matters of concern that the Consulate of the Republic of Sudan was raising. All that he did was to ask the Consulate to give him the address of the Embassy of South Sudan. Thereafter, I came to note that, although they knew that I am from South Sudan they took me to the Embassy of Sudan because they didn't know the location of the South Sudanese Embassy. When we arrived in the South Sudanese Embassy, we were welcome by Victor Makur and Ajing and other officials came also to greet us. There, there is nothing to discuss since I am the man, as Ajing put it clearly to the South African Immigration official that, "This is our man." He went ahead asking the South African immigration officials about the deportation arrangement and offered to cover the ticket fares, as well as for other arrangements, in case if I could be escorted by South African Authority.

I kept quiet, but praying in my heart, for God to do a Miracle of saving me in that time when my life was in total danger. Of course, in that same minute, God did the Miracle. This other South African immigration officer tried to remove my Passport size photograph in order to give to Victor so that, they could process Emergency Travel Document for me that same time, he could not find my photograph.

What happened to my photos which they had taken early in the morning at the centre before they brought me to the Embassy? They never forgot it back in the office at Lindeal. However, Victor told them, "Since you have misplaced the photo, the embassy can arrange for that." The other immigration officer noticed something wrong with the eagerness of the South Sudanese officials in the embassy. He told them that, they would take me along and bring me the following day. To show the wonders of God, these missing photos appeared when we returned back to Lindela. There, I came to believe that God is a God of Miracles and in whatsoever situation one is going through, never lose hope even at the last minute because a miracle can still happen, if it pleases God. In fact, at the embassy by then when we were about to depart, Victor called one of the Immigration officers outside and gave him some money, not knowing that I was watching the transaction through the glass window. However, this officer seemed to be badly greedy for money. Instead of waiting, he immediately called the colleague to come outside, maybe to share the money. However, this other one glanced at him and talked in their local language, which I couldn't understand. Then this same Victor, to show how stupid he was, came inside and told this other guy who remained with me in a soft voice, "I gave something for the two of you with your colleague." When we came out, they were very happy, with the exception of me, the worried soul who had nothing to do to save himself other than to wait upon God for a Miracle. Of course, I couldn't reason why the embassy gave them money.

When you believe in God, never lose hope in any situation because no matter, what it is, you must know that, your God is a God that never absconds or disowns you when you need Him, as long as you know, you are in a good relationship with your God.

Therefore, I knew that whatsoever will happen to me, either deportation or release, it would happen according to the plans of God towards me. I surrendered myself and the situation to Him, and because He is a faithful God of Miracles, my release was a miracle. I never expected the miracle because a miracle is never a miracle if nothing happens to you by surprise. It was at 3 p.m. when the Home Affairs official came into my cell and told me to pack my belongings because I was going. I never asked any question because I thought it was deportation. I was then informed by one of the managers at the Lindela that, I was released under the instruction of the Deputy Director-General of Home Affairs. I went home and the following day, I raised the matter of my asylum permit with the Director-General of Home Affairs but was unsuccessful. Hence I became convinced once again that, the missing of my file from the database of Home Affairs, as well as the misplacement of my passport by the home affairs official, was done intentionally. Hence, the Home Affairs was unwillingly to extend before and even reissue me with asylum permit after my release from the detention facility. Therefore, in this World, never ever try to play any political game against your country when in a refuge, especially when you are not sure of the country where you are because anything can happen to you. Politics is fit only if the ground is properly levelled. Hence, you need to level your ground better and secure the protection and support of key individuals wherever you are, in order to play the game Otherwise, you will end up being a victim of your own political activities and philosophy because politics is a deadly game.

But I shall not hate

I may not be happy with you; I may not like something about you, but I shall not hate

Life is never fair sometimes, but to those who claim to be living in spiritual sights they will say; *"everything works for good to those who love Him (God)"*. That means whether good or bad things happen, one must be receptive because it happens as God allows it to happen. My accusation as a terrorist cost me so much, and it has every smidgen of negative brunt on my life – which also feinted every morsel of my plans. The worst of it was definitely, the kismet of my asylum status and deportation threats that made me leave and wander in search of protection and a place to call home again.

The accusation of terrorism cost me much pain as my life was at the edge. I encountered challenges to earn a living, and to survive from State indefinite detentions without due process as in the normal case of terrorism charges so as to give more time for investigations. There is that deep pain inside me - the pain of betrayal; the pain of not knowing who to trust and call a brother or a friend; the pain of self-denial not to associate with people anymore. But then, there is that realization that I need people if only I have to be happy in life. I can never live my life all alone by myself in this world and expect to be happy. Therefore, whether people give me happiness or sufferings; I shall live my life, and be the original me as God has created, and that is my weapon to destroy the spirit of antagonism, and to bring every enemy down to the understanding of their very own iniquities.

Of course, every pain that comes our way comes with a new realization of facts of life, and all my pains made me to realize that, when people cause you pain, they are simply making you a strong-hearted person, and to be receptive to life with all its challenges, as well as to live a life that is appreciable by the society surrounding you. This is possible only if, you turn the pains into peace with yourself and others – especially those who caused you the pains.

Therefore, the worst mistake that one can make is to hate because hatred never solves any problem. It only inspires the spirit of revenge and can sometimes endanger our human relations with our society that are not by any means partakers in our problems. Even if others wronged against you, never hate them because hatred is an act of evil, which is against God's principle of forgiveness. When you hate, you are giving an opportunity to the devil to rule over your attitudes and actions which in turn will produce the spirit of retributions that can affect your human relationship with the society. Hence, they gave me sufferings and I gave them peace in return and this brought them to acknowledge their own at that dark moment of my life. They turned to be there for me. It was the same Isaac who made it possible for me to leave South Africa by providing me air ticket; and the same man who telephoned Prof. Joseph who became the only contact person in South Africa by then trying to follow up with my case – though he was afraid, and didn't want any person from South Sudan to know that, he was trying to help me to get me free and not extradited.

While Samuel telephoned me and offered for any assistance I just told him that, some other friends were following my case because there was nothing much he could do in this regards, and by then, he was also travelling back to South Sudan where he did some works for National Security with South Sudanese Government of the SPLA/ M. It was here I was convinced that, no enemy is permanent and no friendship is permanent in this world. No one can be your enemy and continue to plan evil against you – if you are not bad. People can conceive an evil against you, but if you remain good toward them, and give that love that God commands us to do, that is to love your enemy, he who that is against you, will turn and be for you in time of your trouble. Your Love for those who wronged against you and your quick desire to forgive those who wrong against you will turn those who are against you, to be the sources of your salvation. Isaac became the only person I depended on mostly for help and whom after I departed South Africa, covered for my upkeeps in Nairobi. He became a true brother – whom I turned to trust with my own life.

Though we never talked about what had happened, I can see the sign of regret in his face, a feeling of deep sorrow and a new spirit for me. Man is not permanently evil by nature, any evil that comes from a man is an influence of circumstances and therefore, man can change to be good because a man has the power to change himself, in life. You don't have to take anyone as a bad person for the rest of their life because of that one or a few bad things they have done to you. There will be that time when they won't do that bad thing to you, but rather do you right and good things at the time you never expected.

Your enemy could be your saviour and your friend could be your enemy, so take man always as God's creature that God can turn to use for your own benefit.

The Death of my Mother

At the time of my birth, I never saw your face, and at the time of your death, I never saw your face too. I can't remember how you look like to
This very day; but all I can remember is your undying love as best mother in the World.

It was very early in the morning when I got an awakening telephone call from my uncle, Kenneth Hussein Jacob while I was still on the bed. After a few seconds of conversations, he asked whether I got a telephone call from my elder sister, Vivian Lucy Martin? I replied, "No, but I talked with them three days ago." Uncle then told me that, last night my mother was not feeling well and was taken to the hospital; unfortunately, she could not make it. So she passed away that morning at 5 a.m. I took a deep breath without any word to him and then dropped the phone.

At first, I had that hardened heart. There were never tears – but then, they started to flow down uncontrollably. Those were tears of love for a mother, caused not by the death because I knew we will all die - but by the pain of her suffering for me and the manner, she died without me having done anything great for her. Her death was another painful experience. Indeed, even if we are used to death each moment death occurs in the family, there is that fresh pain and sorrow in our hearts. My mother and I never stayed together for long because at the age of 12, I was already far away from her but I am always connected to her in heart, mind and spirit.

Therefore, her memories are so close to my heart and have been there in me throughout my life, though far away from her, until now.

The Memories of her drying my tears, and comforting me when I was a child, the memories of her voices speaking to me and above all, the memories of her prayers as she asked God, to take care of me when things were not good for me. These were great and unforgettable memories of how great a mother is, and how dear she will always be for you as her child.

It was really painful to lose a mother and for me, it was really worse because she died at the time when I was in serious insecurity problems where my life was in danger – without hope for life – though having faith that, my God will protect and save me that time. Apart from these threats, I was also broke by then and I just didn't know how to help in monetary terms so that she would get a decent burial even if I would not attend her burial. I phoned my elder sister. When she was given the phone, she said to me, "Mother is gone, but be strong – we are now all well, just be strong," I just couldn't bear her saying that. There came fresh tears more than ever and I dropped the phone. The death of my mother caused me real confusion and it was another dark day - in that black moment of my life where I was surrounded by threats. It was unbelievable for a mother who suffered for you, who worked so hard to raise you up to be a grown-up in the society, and just dying without enjoying the fruits of her child. The day I received the news of her death, all I could do was to imagine, how she suffered for us, how she worked hard to ensure we get every basic thing we needed; and could feel her pain and feelings at the time I was detained and warranted with extradition.

My tears could not cease because of the memories of her sleepless nights especially when I was in detention awaiting my extradition and whenever I had that opportunity to talk to her on phone. She would tell me, *"You are my son, I gave birth to you and raised you as a man today; God will listen to my humble cry as mother, God will see my suffering and therefore, nothing harmful will happen to you, you will be free in the Name of Jesus Christ."* She would, as usual, tell me to trust in God, to put God first and never to forget praying because it is only God, who would help. Indeed, her prayers worked and I saw the miracle of God at that time as I said in the previous chapter, my release was a miracle because I never expected that I would be released.

That was my darling mother, my prayer warrior and the person I always turned to when things were not good for me. She was all that I had in my life and she just died without me seeing her for 13 years, and even without paying her for everything she had done for me. In my every struggle, I had that dream by then that God would one day bless me and all I wanted was to make my mother happy and proud. However, that was just a dream, because life is different from the dream of our hearts and the thoughts of our minds. We can plan and dream and there is no question about that, but only God who makes us see our dreams and plans coming into existence. Therefore, it is good to plan with God than to make our own plans because God is the solid foundation for every dreams and plan of man. I had my own plans about how I wanted to make my mother happy and proud, but then God also had His own plans and because God is all-powerful and the master of every life, He won.

I just lost because life is not a plan but what happens as we live the life while the real designer, (God) allows us to go through from each phase of life in order to get to the real side that He alone determined for us, but not what we determined for ourselves.

Of course, the pain is not because I wanted mother again in my life – to raise me up and feed me like when I was a child. I am already big and it is supposed to be my turn to do the things she did to me as a child- to do for her as Magogo. She died at the time when, if I were to be fast in getting married, I would have married and gave her grandchildren too. I have no problem because I know we will all die one day but the pain is that, what is it that my mother benefitted from me before she died as a mother who suffered and raised me up? Besides all, it is 13 years that I never saw her and that really makes me feel like a careless man, a man who never thinks and cares for the person who made him the man he is today. I felt a useless person – but, I knew that my mother was an understanding mother at all times who cared more about my safety and success than anything else that I could do for her. I remember the time she was already sick and I was thinking of coming at that time, she sent me a message not to come because she was afraid of my security. Yes, I was already a big man but what about my siblings? How would they cope up with the experience of her death which they had never experienced before? How would they cope up with a life without a mother that they are so used to? This is the frustration that is caused by the reality of life when death occurs. I have that hope that is always accompanied by faith that, God won't let us down - no matter what situation we are going through; because He is the God that works according to His own plans.

We can't influence Him to do things for us according to our will. We can't influence God in His decisions because if we could, then God ceases to be God. If we can influence God to do things for us as we want, we will never trust, obey and praise God, but will be rebellious to His word because we know that, when we need him, we will influence him to come to our aid and that will reduce Him from being God to an object that we can play around with. God's plans are always great for us; we can't influence His plans but by being obedient and trusting in him, our obedience and trust make us be persistent through all kinds of situations until God comes to our aid. I remembered one day my elder sister phoned me and after a long conversation, she said to me, *"God is helping many other people, and one day, He will help us too."* There is a time for everything and in whatsoever situation one is going through, don't forget that, God never forgets you, He is there and will always be there for you.

The *Life Mania* is the story of my life that was opened by the death of my father and closed by the death of my mother but my life's journey is not over. The *Life Mania* defines me as I journey to the unknown world of life and death, Heaven and hell, success and failure. As you close it and put it down, remember you have not yet closed and put my life on the shelf because I am still on my journey.

About the Author

John Sunday Martin is an advocate for national unity, democratic reformation and sustainable development, within the context of a multi-cultural South Sudan. He maintains a strong belief in the positive power of patriotism as an antidote to the crippling parochialism that has handicapped the nation since independence.

He was born in 1981 in a remote township of Amadi in South Sudan. He grew up as an orphan and joined the Sudan People's Liberation Army Movement (SPLA/M) at a young age. He rose through the military ranks during the course of the long civil war, which eventually led to the independence of the Republic of South Sudan.

John Sunday Martin went on to serve as a spokesman for the Revolutionary Movement of National Salvation (REMNASA); an armed resistance front led by Major General Lasuba Ladoru Wango, prior to its formal amalgamation with the SPLA - In Opposition (SPLA-IO) under the leadership of Dr. Riek Machar.

www.ingramcontent.com/pod-product-compliance
Lightning Source LLC
Chambersburg PA
CBHW020327010526
44107CB00054B/2006